Franco Archibugi

Planning Theory
From the Political Debate
to the Methodological Reconstruction

Franco Archibugi

Planning Theory

From the Political Debate
to the Methodological Reconstruction

 Springer

FRANCO ARCHIBUGI
c/o Planning Studies Centre
Via Federico Cassitto 110
00134 Roma
Italy

planning.studies@tiscali.it

Library of Congress Control Number: 2007929930

ISBN 978-88-470-0695-9 Springer Milan Berlin Heidelberg New York

Springer is a part of Springer Science+Business Media

springer.com

© Springer-Verlag Italia 2008

Printed in Italy

Cover design: Simona Colombo, Milano
Typesetting: LE-TEX Jelonek, Schmidt & Vöckler GbR, Leipzig, Germany
Printing and binding: Grafiche Porpora, Segrate (MI)

Springer-Verlag Italia – Via Decembrio 28 – I-20137 Milano

Printed on acid-free paper

Preface

This book has re-elaborated, in a unified and organic way, some of my contributions to the academic debates among European and American planning "theorists".

Such contributions were born in relation to my participation at a conference on planning theory promoted by Oxford Brookes University, in April 1998. This conference[1] gave me a very interesting opportunity to be among other scholars on the subject. On this occasion I had the opportunity to pour out, into the bosom of an abundant group of colleagues (to whom I am bound together by some years of scientific contact on the issues of the effectiveness and methods of planning), my concerns about the turns taken by the literature of planning theory over the last decade or more[2]. The substance of my concerns has been revisited in Chap. 1 of this book.

However, in the current criticism of planning theory's trends, I soon realized that my demands for a more advanced integration of the different approaches to planning, and particularly of improved integration between the procedural approach and the "substantive" approach, was not yet sufficiently clear and perceptible. So I looked again at reformulating, in a positive way, my ideas about the turn which, in my opinion, the theoretical and methodological planning studies should have to take in order to obtain an operational relaunch of planning itself, on a more advanced scientific basis (avoiding, however, slipping into technicalities that become useless and misleading when not used for the benefit of a clear and consistent method)[3].

---

[1] *Planning Theory Conference*, Oxford Brookes University, 2–4 April 1998.

[2] A further paper with the same arguments has been also published in *European Planning Studies*, Vol. 12, No. 3, April 2004.

[3] This reconsideration and awareness has been helped by very accurate and pertinent comments and criticism received from my colleagues E.R. Alexander, John Bryson, Giuseppe De Luca, Seymour Mandelbaum, and Niraj Verma. The critical comments of Verma, with which I largely agree and for which I am very grateful, have been made only on the papers that have formed the basis of Chap. 1. He concluded that my first contribution needed a section that showed why the integration between socio-economic forecasting and other connections that I anticipated should be implemented. I think such connections, their description, and their motivations, deserve and need much more than a section! They constitute the proper subject, the proper matter, of planning theory. This does not exclude, but confirms, the idea

Thus, I wanted to integrate that first contribution with a further description of the possible linking of procedural planning and various "substantive" aspects of planning by means of a *unitary methodological scheme*, which has become the object of this book[4].

I tried therefore:

–   to delimit the traditional fields which until now have progressed separately and in open order, at most with some interdisciplinary cooperation of a technical nature,

---

that if they are not well described in some ways, even provisionally (as Verma requested), my claims are not even properly understood, because they lack clear references and examples. This has induced me to take a new step towards the description of those connections (even if I think it not yet sufficient).

Alexander's criticisms helped me to perceive the seriousness of the absence of a systemic vision of planning theory to which we refer ourselves, and to incite me to risk the defect of excessive schematism, but not to take for granted and acknowledge some arguments too easily! I hope that the corrections I have made, which are more formal than substantial, will satisfy Alexander, whose severe critiques I have always found stimulating, even when I have not agreed with them.

The Mandelbaum's comments were nearly all pertinent and I appreciated his kind suggestions, even on texts, like mine, which were very far from his own approach and writing style. I am aware, however, of the difficulty of adequately taking into account his viewpoint and to use his ideas in a way that conforms to their potential quality. I sense that his historical perception of planning pushes him towards a vision of planning theory very different from mine, and my efforts to reconstruct a field and a method appropriate for planning theory go in a direction very different from his own.

To John Bryson and to his friendly comments on my effort, I owe a sincere gratitude; however, he also cheerfully pressed me to use less polemical arguments, arguing very rightly that sometimes this might be an obstacle, instead of facilitating the understanding and the forming of a common consensus. I have agreed and applied his general advice and from the still remaining polemical phrasing, the reader can appreciate how useful and necessary his recommendations were… Finally, I owe it to Giuseppe De Luca that this book has been equipped with a brief chapter of 'conclusions'. To Stefano Moroni, I owe the hard effort to review and synthetize, in the journal *Planning Theory*, the Italian edition of this book that allowed me to revisit some passages of it.

To these colleagues, and to others with whom I have associated through many years of attempting to implement a contact network for the progress in the theoretical discourse on planning science and an improved determinateness in planning theory, I am very grateful for help given to me.

[4] Thus, this book is a further step (still very approximate) toward the already announced ongoing work on the foundations of a *general planning methodology*. I must say that in the effort to achieve (as suggested by comments mentioned above) within the substantive field, the needed change of approach, the first routes and thematisms of a new integrated (or unified) discipline of planning (see Chaps. 2 to 5 of this book) I have amply used a paper presented to the 1st World Congress on Planning Science, promoted in Palermo (Italy) by *Planning Studies Centre*, with the support of UNESCO, the United Nations University (Tokyo), the European University Institute (Florence), and the (Italian) National Research Council (CNR). (That paper has been published in: *Socio-Economic Planning Sciences, International Journal* in 1996, vol. 30, N. 2, pp. 81–102.)

and that should engage themselves in the "integration" in a new unified methodology (Chap. 2);

- to discuss the merits and limits of a transdisciplinary methodological integration, based on a "programming" approach instead of the *positivistic* approach, which has until now been dominant in planning researches and activities (Chap. 3);
- to outline the first routes of the new discipline (procedural scheme for the selection of plans, interrelationship between different "levels" of planning, institutional procedures of plans bargaining, and consulting system on preference, information, monitoring and plan evaluation) (Chap. 4);
- to list some proper integrative topics of the new discipline (Chap. 5).

All this then flows together, in Chap. 6, to form the outline of an *operational logical framework*, through which are integrated and unified, with an exhaustive and complete methodology, all types, forms, and procedures of planning[5].

I then focused on one of the most neglected (but, at the same time, one of the most important, if not *the* most important) "levels" of planning for a process of methodological integration like the one pursued here: the "national" level (Chap. 7 of the book)[6].

Lastly, I closed this first effort by pointing out the basic elements of an integrative planning methodology, with some considerations on what I would call the "pitfalls" or "traps" (in experiments I have performed) of any type of *plan evaluation* (Chap. 8)[7].

Plan evaluation being the "other side of the coin" to every work of planning, any integrative effort brought on the planning methods immediately has a specular effect in the evaluation process.

Since planning has been applied until today without systemic control and coordination, and without the said *integrative and unified methodology*, this is, in my opinion, the major cause of the very poor and disappointing (not to mention substantially erroneous and misleading) plan evaluations.

Therefore, that is the cause of planning failure itself, i.e., of the plans that collapsed at the first test of their compatibility and consistency with the context of planning itself.

Acknowledgements and Dedication

This book is dedicated to some outstanding colleagues with whom I have maintained personal contact and useful debating in the "planning theory" field. They are: Ernest R.

---

[5] A first version of this framework has been presented to the colleagues at the great unitary "World Planning School Congress" promoted by the planning school academic associations: European (AESOP), American (ASCP), Asiatic (ASPA) and Australian and New-Zealander (ANZAPS), in Shanghai, China, July 11–15, 2001.

[6] This chapter employs a paper already presented to the XII Aesop Congress, 22–25 July 1998 in Aveiro (Portugal).

[7] This chapter utilizes a paper presented at an academic meeting in March 2001 at the London University College (Bartlett School) to honour Nathaniel Lichfield, as "father" of the "plan's evaluation".

Alexander, Phil Cooke, Andreas Faludi, John Forester, Patsy Healey, Nathaniel Lichfield, Seymour Mandelbaum, Luigi Mazza, Francesco Domenico Moccia, Stefano Moroni, Giorgio Piccinato, Niraj Verma. I am thankful to them to have stimulated my reflection on this topic, both when our feelings and opinions were converging and when they were diverging.

The English text has been revised from many contributors, according the different stages of the individual papers here merged. To recall all of them it would be very difficult. The last of them has been Robert Redman. The final copyeditor by Springer was Jardi Mullinax. Thanks for all.

Contents

1

Planning Theory: Reconstruction or Requiem?

1.1 A Certain Uneasiness about "Planning Theory"

In spite of the geometric progression in the quantity of scholars who have devoted themselves (more or less totally) to *theoretical* reflections about planning, both as a practice and as an academic discipline (to the point of founding a new strand or discipline of study, *Planning Theory*)[1], I think that a diffuse, creeping uneasiness has pervaded all the participants of this discipline. This uneasiness concerns not only the role, the sense, and the boundaries of Planning Theory, but also those of planning *tout court*. I would even be tempted to say that, paradoxically, this wide reflection and debate about planning (called *Planning Theory*) has worsened, instead of improving, the uncertainties and 'derangement' of planning itself, both as practice and profession.

How can this have been?

To use a metaphor (which has been perhaps abused, and is perhaps abusive), it is as if, confronted with a dark pond (planning) in which objects at the bottom can be seen only in an obscure, deformed way, people are throwing stones (planning theory) into the pond, in the hope of being able to clarify and better define the objects. Instead, all they are accomplishing is to muddy the situation further and make comprehension impossible. After continuing in this manner for some time, these people become discouraged and arrive at the conclusion that either:

a. (for some people) it will never be possible to discern the objects clearly;
b. (for others) the act of clarifying the pond creates new situations of darkness, subject to analogous uncertainties; or,
c. (for the remaining few) there is no need to make the pond any clearer[2].

---

[1] Consolidated through university course offerings, academic journals, congresses, and even academic associations.

[2] At the risk of being irreverent, it seems to me that the planning theory debate has arrived at something similar to these conclusions (see also some alternative interesting considerations on this subject in Taylor 1984, and Simmie 1989). As a general reappraisal of the debate on planning theory, I recommend the collections of papers edited by Burchell and Sterlieb (1978) and by Healey et al. (1982). As tools, the readings in planning theory edited by Chris Paris (1982) and Scott Campbell and Susan S. Fenstein (2003).

In this chapter, I will try to further develop that initial reflection (with the unavoidable risk of contributing to the creation of further confusion) by trying to determine whether the voluminous reflection and debate within planning theory has led to a better understanding of the meaning of "planning" and a clarification of its role, and if the response to this question is negative (as I would suspect), I will try to examine:

– what the reasons are for the situation in which we find ourselves; and
– under what conditions a further development of the debate (which we could still call, without hesitation, *Planning Theory*) can achieve a real contribution to what should be its chief objectives: *the better understanding of the meaning of planning and of helping to perfect its methods.*

1.2 Have We Improved the Clarity of Planning Methodology?

I would first like to revive, but with a slightly different meaning, the classical distinction (by Andreas Faludi, the scholar who has contributed more than anyone else to the animation of the wide reflection on planning) between theory *of* planning and theory *in* planning[3]. My argument will be that instead of the two-fold development of planning theory (*of* or *in*), an explosion has been produced of a sort of theory *on* planning (or *about* planning) which has been the cause of the poor results obtained by the former. In other words, developments in the theory *on* planning have prevented any real progress in the theories *of* and *in* planning.

Faludi's initial work on this subject has been very useful, or at least, it had the potential to be useful. It was a great effort to summarise, in an organic or systemic way, all of the issues emerging from the practice of planning, and the lack of co-ordination among the many different approaches and directions developed during the 1950s and 1960s[4]. If Faludi's work had been called *The Logic of/in Planning*, it appropriately could remain as the foundation of an operational concept of planning, a sort of introduction to planning as practice, and given its general validity (its applicability to all types of planning), it would have the capacity to become an advanced tool for operational awareness for the whole field of planning.

As such, Faludi's work could have kept its place as the foundation for many educational curricula in planning matters (physical, economic, and social). In others words, it could have continued to maintain the role of an introduction to the elaboration of the plan (of any scale or type), and to the plan's *implementation*.

Instead, Faludi's work has been received and commented on as an essay of political philosophy, an occasion to develop reflections (*generaliter*) on the relationships between *political science* and that particular field of political operation, the *development plan* (mainly in the urban field). In this guise, Faludi's work fostered the development of considerations *on* planning which became an object of discussion as an

---

[3] Faludi, 1973a, p. 21.

[4] Of course Faludi's work was a product of its time. It profited from many other works oriented in the same direction (McLoughlin, Chadwick, etc.). The companion book of readings, edited by Faludi himself, is a good example of the wide context of a "planning theory" as the logical reorganisation of the practice of planning in several directions (Faludi, ed. 1973b).

end in itself, rather than as a means of introducing new and improved methods of planning (see, for instance Ph. Allmendinger, 2002).

Starting from the work of Faludi (and others), it was possible and appropriate to patiently and carefully develop the construction of the components, materials, and elements of a new building, the renovated discipline of planning, as *science* and as *practice*. It would be helpful to discuss, describe and define the supports of such a new discipline or science, the load bearing walls, the trusses, the floors, the stairways (one or more?) to communicate between floors, the rooms and other spaces on the floors with their functions, the flexibility of use of various rooms, the passages, and hallways to assure both independence and communication. Furthermore, on a more operational scale, it would be suitable to deepen the consistency of different methods and approaches, in order to assure order and stability, sustainability, and the survival of the building of planning itself.

Unfortunately, very little of this has been done. Every single element of the building has been discussed by itself, forgetting its function in relation to the whole. Even the interrelationships among various parts or facets of the planning "building" have been analysed on a case-by-case basis, according to a limited (too limited) scope. These analyses have ignored the general scope of the planning "building" as defined by its comprehensive design.

Missing what should be their proper mission, the planning theorists (who deserve this name, it seems to me, only in that they should engage themselves in *methods* and *techniques*, and not in *philosophical talkativeness*) have forsaken the planning practitioners (who should be, first of all, their pupils), without supporting them, at least in their formative stage, with disciplinary *know-how* and *rules*, with a behavioural code, i.e., with basic guidelines, instructions and warnings.

Left to themselves, *practitioners* have "practised" planning without order and rules, without any analysis of consistency with the "environment" and real consciousness of the "constraints" or the "resources", contravening even the most elementary requirements of planning: i.e., order, rules and consistency[5]. Should we be surprised, then, if the practice of planning has such poor internal consistency and low esteem outside the profession? I do not know (because I am not so familiar with geometry) whether this kind of planning deserves to be called *Euclidean* or *non-Euclidean*. But I do know for certain that it would horrify any good father of the scientific method (say Galileo Galilei, for instance). Respect for a *scientific* approach by planning the-

---

[5] By "consistency", I mean the capacity of a plan feature or decision to fit with environmental constraints that are beyond and outside the delimitation of the system or unit under planning. I recall one clamorous example of this kind of inconsistency from Italy: some decades ago, a research project of the Planning Studies Centre tried to extrapolate the whole pattern of the individual demographic forecasting drawn from the existing (master) plans of Italian municipalities (around half of the approximately 7,000 which exist in all of Italy), through an appropriately weighted evaluation. The result was that around the year 2000 Italy should shelter 400 million inhabitants! You can imagine what other results, in terms of capital investment, infrastructure, housing, land use, etc, were reached. Who can assert (honestly) that this sounds only like a typical Italian case? (Archibugi 1980).

orists would render plans more consistent (i.e., more *rational*) and, therefore, more feasible and implementable. *Rationality* can be identified with *reality*[6].

Rationality which is not identified with reality, is not truly rationality. It is a pseudo-rationality. At the same time, however realistic and feasible, plans cannot exactly coincide with reality, which must be *ex-post* or historical. Plans try to have an impact on this reality; they intend to govern and possibly modify it. Otherwise what kind of plans would they be?

In these (*ex-ante*) terms plans must be "irrealist". As with the French saying, "*C'est stupide d'être plus royaliste que le roi*", the planner's saying is: "*No reason to be more realist than reality itself*". The best (*ex ante*) realism is the replication of reality (so beloved by the model-builders) and consequently any plan at all. According to certain current tenors of planning theory, this sounds like the implicit conclusion of its obsession with "realism".

Moreover, it is obvious that there will always be an imperfection in the implementation of plans. This fact, however, does not prevent plans from being useful, or even necessary, if we wish to obtain results. In a certain sense, plans are not made to be implemented, but rather to be instruments for enlightening decisions and actions, preventing them from being taken in darkness. The more rational the plan (the more it takes account of reality and its complexity), the more it has a chance to be successful in the creation of conditions suitable for the achievement of its objectives.

1.3 What Are the Reasons for the Deceiving Development of Planning Theory?

I suspect that the origin of the deceiving development of planning theory is to be found in an equivocal (and apparently well based) extension of its field.

I will try to explain (as well as I can) what I mean, evoking an early, elementary, unsophisticated reference to and justification of planning theory by E.C. Banfield:

> The word "planning" is given a bewildering variety of meanings. To some it means socialism. To others the layout and design of cities. To still others regional development schemes like TVA, measures to control the business cycles, or 'scientific management' in industry. It would be easy to overemphasise what these activities have in common; their differences are certainly more striking than their similarities. Nevertheless, it may be that there is a method of making decisions which is to some extent common to all these fields and to others as well and that the logical structure of this method can usefully be elaborated as a theory of planning (Banfield 1959).

I think that if planning theory had limited its field to this concept, to the "*method of making decisions which is to some extent common to all fields*" and to the "*logical structure of this method*", then developments in planning theory could have advanced further, and planning could have rescued itself from its widespread failure. This is

---

[6] As any scholar who has a certain, modest familiarity with the course of philosophical thinking (from Plato to Aristotle, Kant to Hegel) knows well, only in a vulgar (not really philosophical) version of our language is the *rationalist* in opposition to the *realist*.

not so far from Faludi's earlier effort to give to planning theory its own proper field, distinct from the various applications of planning (which he called *substantive* planning) and to push planners, who, I suppose, should come from all kinds of substantive planning (but, unfortunately, this has not been the case), to occupy themselves with the "*common*" aspect, which he called "*procedural*". In this way, as is known, Faludi risked creating a sort of excessive division between a theory *of* planning and a theory *in* planning. He paraphrased Britton Harris' expression (which I too consider very important): "We have great need of a science *of* planning in order to determine what is science *in* planning".

1.3.1 The Equivocal Case of the "Substantive" Side of Planning Theory

However, the way in which Faludi chose to restrain planning theory to the first aspect (the procedural concept of planning), leaving the second (the different cases of substantive planning), has probably also been a misleading factor. In doing so, he risked renouncing too much in order to establish strict connections between the procedural and substantive aspects, and to establish a permanent, integrated interrelationship between different forms of substantive plans, just (as considered in the Harris phrase) "to determine *what is science in planning*". (Let me quote also some forgotten writings by Britton Harris' writings on this argument, 1967 and 1977.)

This division, which Faludi indeed never practised[7], has probably been at the root of the fact that planning theory, instead of becoming a theory *of* planning including the difficult problem of defining *interrelationships* between procedural and substantive planning, has become a sort of theory *on* planning (in the sense that will be developed below); and, moreover, a theory on planning which is limited mainly to the experience of town planners, missing the involvement of planners of other substantive plans.

Anyhow, while Faludi elaborated a clear and fruitful theory of planning on the side of planning theory (which I am frankly reluctant to call only "procedural"[8]), the further developments of planning theory have been directed in a relatively disordered way, in a fashion that has missed the benefits of Faludi's effort. In other words,

---

[7] In effect, Faludi stated that the distinction between theory *in* planning and theory *of* planning (the latter being planning theory) should not result in an entirely separate development of the two; and also that "clearly, both types of theory are needed for effective planning". He also stated that "planners should view procedural theory as forming an envelope around substantive theory, rather than vice versa". But independently from the question about which should be the "envelope" of the other, the main focus of his book (and of further works), has been the *procedural* and (later) the *epistemological* aspect of the planning knowledge and action (see also Faludi 1986, 1987 and 1989), as a process, and poor attention to the substantive interrelations among different aspects of planning. Anyhow, Faludi provided a very important contribution towards clarifying the procedural aspects of planning, and towards formulating the foundations of a theory of planning in its substantive aspects. It is not his fault if the further development of the theory of planning has not taken this direction.

[8] Because many of the topics of Faludi's book deal with methodological aspects of planning that have a substantial validity in the preparation of plans, i.e., in their substantive capacity to be effective and feasible in their contents and not only in their procedure or implementation.

I have the sense that the major themes that have occupied the literature of planning theory in the last three decades, for instance: rationality or rationalism in planning; the operationality of the planning mind, subject, agent or agency; the logical foundations of planning behaviour, and all the opposing approaches or methodologies usually discussed, blueprint versus processual outcome, comprehensive-deductive versus disjointed-incrementalist approaches, normative versus functional mode, environmental and contextual styles of planning, etc., were exhaustively covered in Faludi's work, and found little improvement later in switching to what I consider a useless theory *on* planning.

1.3.2 Expanding the Scope Too Much

The main misleading factor, as already stated, remains the excessive extension given to the scope of planning theory. John Friedmann, the author of the well-known impressive encyclopaedic treatise about planning (in the public domain), in the introductory chapter of his work, precisely devoted to the "terrain of planning theory"[9], after a very interesting and extended reasoning about market rationality and social rationality, the uses of planning, the relations between planning and the political order, and other remarks, does not give us any definition of the *terrain* or the subject-matter of planning theory. On the contrary he concludes that:

> a comprehensive exploration of the terrain of planning theory must cull from all the relevant disciplines those elements that are central to an understanding of planning in the public domain. The theory of planning is an eclectic field, bounded by political philosophy; epistemology; macro-sociology; neo-classical and institutional economics; public administration; organisation development; political sociology; anarchist, Marxist, and utopian literature[10] (Friedmann 1987, pp. 39–40).

We can however ask ourselves if this "eclectic field" should not be the same as other research strands different from planning theory. This doesn't help us to better define the specific subject of planning theory and it also makes sense to ask ourselves if such reasoning, under the headline of *planning theory*, developed over an expanse of such vast boundaries, origins and "mines", could be at the root of the regretted *loss of identity* of planning theory itself. About the "quest for identity" see William Salet (1980).

Nobody intends to deny that the planning theorist, as well as the planner, possesses and cultivates his own cultural background and has roots in a vast range of strands, works and even academic disciplines (going under several more or less conventional and innovative headlines). However, this occurs for everybody, not solely for the planning theorist, and the mere (full or partial) list of possible sources from which planning theorists can draw does not help us to understand, or better define, his or her own

---

[9] Friedmann, 1987, Part 1.

[10] And given the vast boundaries attributed to this "eclectic field", I don't understand why we should exclude, in his opinion, other disciplines (see footnote 16), such as: "psychology, cultural anthropology, geography, history, political science, micro-sociology, and the humanities, including design theory".

terrain of work: terrain that he or she has to cultivate in a specific way, to justify the formation of a new discipline. From this eclecticism does not arise a more precise definition of this terrain, as, for instance, from Banfield's scant phrase (which the unceasing adorers of novelty would define, without real justification, as "old" or archaic). From this cultivated eclecticism, only confusion arises, and frequently, also superficiality.

If planning theory can not even succeed in defining itself and its object, and if an endless series of definitional possibilities from different points of view are left open, how can it help us to get a more precise definition of planning *tout court* (which should be one of its first tasks)?

And, if we do not succeed in getting a more precise definition of planning, how shall we stop planning activities from reducing themselves to an endless "telling of stories"[11] (territorial, sectorial, historical), without any intrinsic connection, without any method of reading, without any elementary instruction or regulation, without any "principle", "foundation" or methodological "primer", in short, without any of those ingredients which in any field of knowledge mark the difference between a practised approach (based on so called "experience") and science or professionalism? Do we not run the risk of transforming planning (and our planning conferences) from a profession (of the arts or sciences, as we prefer) into a wide literary bazaar?

Is all this "rationalism"? It seems to me only common sense[12].

---

[11] It is not by chance that an explicit trend, and for this reason much more consequential and consistent than other equivocal manifestations of a generalizing politology on planning, to see the task of the "theorist" (a disconcerting thesis for one who is bound to the Greco-Roman etymons, but anyhow suggestive) as limited to that of "telling stories," in the conviction that "planning arguments are characteristically expressed as stories. As they both tell and manage these stories, planners maintain and redesign communities" (Mandelbaum 1992); or the task is that of "reading plans" as they are developed and located in the urban history (Mandelbaum 1990, 1993), and it is not by chance that this reduction of the planners' profession to the telling and reading of urban stories and plans ("planners as writers"; "plans as narrative") be sustained by a professor of Urban History. At least in this case people know from the beginning (with clarity, sincerity, and intellectual honesty) what is intended by "planning theory" (see also Throgmorton 1993, 1996). My only divergence is that all this could be named "Urban History"; or, with some reservations, "(Urban) Planning History"; then again, perhaps it could be (although it would be an unsupportable sophistication), "Theory of Planning History"; but certainly not "Planning Theory." And as a final result of those kinds of elaborations, I can discern a product of amusing weekend reading for urban planners (but only for those who have enough sensibility and imaginative acumen to penetrate and understand them as hermetic poetry); but I am scared to consider them as the basis of a professional *know-how* for young professional planner candidates!

[12] This has nothing to do with the *vexata quaestio* of the origins of knowledge and its connection with action. The entire history of philosophy has dealt with this question so extensively that an attempt to deal with it in a few pages would be folly. I persist in following the idea that knowledge and action are intimately related and we have to tailor, to calibrate our cognitive analysis to the definition of our action objectives ("decision-oriented analysis"), and this offers or obliges us to have a certain awareness of the relativity of the planning objectives. But, I repeat, this calls for another level of reasoning, and has nothing to do with my previous sentence. A good reading in such argument has been (in my past) an essay of Hudson and Friedman on "knowledge and action: a guide to planning theory" (1973).

On the other hand, Friedmann himself, in the same chapter on the terrain of planning theory, introduces a series of questions about planning theory which can be considered absolutely appropriate (if settled in systematic and consequential order) to constitute a very interesting syllabus for a discussion of planning theory.

1.3.3 Expanding the Terrain and the Roots

From the vision of the "terrain" or "field" arises the vision of the "roots". It is not surprising that Friedmann speaks about "two centuries of planning theory" (even if in terms of "traditions"). In this historical perspective the problem of reconstructing planning theory from an historical point of view gives us the opportunity to develop a sort of "history of planning theory" and to include within it people and writers that did not at the time have any idea of being the traditional founders of planning theory in its different approaches[13].

Even if a history of two centuries (dating from the age of the "Enlightenment" and of the democratic and industrial revolutions), makes sense given the marked social and economic changes connected with that age, people may be curious to know what strict "rationale" has set aside many other social and political thinkers from the Enlightenment, or from the time immediately before it[14]. But even in this "narrowness", the heritage discovered by planning theory is incredibly vast. According to Friedmann, it embraces the entire history of political economy[15]; it includes all the movements of scientific management[16]; it is identified with all the traditions of sociology as a science[17]; and, as "*social mobilisation*", encompasses all possible socialist thinking.[18]

To sum up, the roots of planning theory are made up of the entirety of the social and political thought of the last two centuries. I do not believe that in these circumstances it could be easy for planning theory to find its own identity.

From this vision, it is not surprising that, under the heading of planning theory, we find people who deal with a huge range of themes, from political science to sociology,

---

[13] This occupies two-thirds of Friedmann's book (Part 2), and even the rest is a continuous coming back to the historical bases (Part 3).

[14] I think, for instance, of the work of Vico, Locke, Hume, Turgot, Rousseau, Kant, Wegelin, Condorcet, to mention the first that come to mind, and which deserve no less than the others to be included in the list of the unaware progenitors of planning theory.

[15] In the approach named as "*policy analysis*": from Adam Smith, to J.S. Mill, Jevons, Walras, Marshall, Pigou, Keynes, until the new "welfare economics", and at the same time all schools of system analysis and engineering, policy science and public policies.

[16] In the approach named "*social learning*": from the engineering method of Frederick Taylor, with derivations from and connections with "Organisation Development (OD), and other issues of educational psychology.

[17] In the approach named as "*social reform*": the entire tradition of sociology from Saint-Simon to Comte, Durkheim, Max Weber, Mannheim, until Popper and even modern American sociology; as well as the entire tradition of institutional economics (from the German historic school to Veblen, Commons, Mitchell), and American pragmatism (James, Dewey).

[18] Encompassing from the Utopians to Marx and Marxists; but also Radicals and Anarchists, until the "Frankfurt School" (Horkheimer, Adorno, Marcuse, Habermas).

from economics to psychology, and also any kind of social movement (liberation of women, or of homosexuals); the same range that we can find under any other heading of knowledge[19].

This is truly the crucial point for the future of planning theory. In order to justify such an expansive field, planning theory must characterise itself with a limited and restrained point of view: actually that of urban planners, *stricto sensu*. Thus planning theory becomes the recreational and hobby field for urban planners ("a few scribbles, for urban planners, on the universe"!).

My idea is that planning theory should be exactly the opposite. It should start with a rigidly restrained field of analysis (planning, in its different applications) and bring to it an enormity of points of view; those points of view have remained until now very separate, to such an extent as to make each one incapable of providing a truly *integrated* and *comprehensive* vision of planning.

The theory of planning should be the result of a permanent exchange of points of view, from planners of different origin and professional extractions, aimed at building a common doctrine and methodology, and a new professionalism.

In this vision are the foundations of a new discipline of planning[20], adapted to the modern conditions of public or community management. This new management increasingly exploits improved know-how concerning the effectiveness of decision-making and "rational" methods, i.e., greater consciousness of the complexity of governance problems.

Therefore, the relationship between, (a) the know-how improved through new integrative methods and, (b) the governmental and community institutions and decision-makers, is an integrative part of the new discipline. This relationship, its development, and its functional articulation can be the *object* of planning theory. But no more than is proper; no more than is necessary in order to make planners the controllers of decision-making consistency and prompters of the limits and constraints in the relationship between different goals and objectives, and between objectives and means, without the risk of becoming decision-makers themselves (as planners, of course; not as citizens).

And again, this vision does not address another issue, recently developed in the planning theory debate: that the planner should even assume decision-making roles and abandon his role of "dead wood" as regarding effective management. This is an old subject, stemming from the common, widespread frustration of planners about the lack of implementation of their plans. But this "implementation problem" has been seen by the true planning methodologists (or planologists) in very different ways than it is seen at the level of practitioners. To make plans effective, they must be, in the first place, *feasible*; and their feasibility comes from their consistency with planning at other levels and their consistency with the environmental conditions. To achieve

---

[19] With this trend we can expect to find soon in our journals (nominally specialised), as turns the wind of fashionable subjects, papers on Christianity, Buddhism, Zionism, the evolution of eroticism, the culinary art, diet issues, bio-ethics, cosmopolitanism and so on: all subjects about which I foster (surely!) a deep and sincere personal interest.

[20] More details on this new discipline, in a paper of mine (Archibugi 1996) resumed in the next Chaps. 3, 4 and 5.

this level of consciousness, the method recommends separating the "selection problem" (in the plan preparation phase) from the "implementation problem" (in the plan management or application phase)[21].The connection must be not simultaneous, but *operational*, that is, it has to follow a pre-defined procedure and provide feedback.

It is surprising that this argument (despite its wide appearance) recurs many times[22] and not necessarily with improved logic.

1.3.4 The Lack of Relationship with "Substantive" Planning

Many authors lay stress not on the vastness of the planning theory field, but only on the many approaches that support it. However, from the best intentions of making students aware of the multidisciplinarity of the approaches to planning theory can arise another dangerous and misleading development of planning theory itself.

For instance, in a very useful introductory textbook on the "approaches to planning", Alexander[23] (rightly concerned about giving content to planning theory) felt that it was not possible to leave out of consideration the meaning and content of planning itself, for which we attempt to develop the "theory", and he stated:

> The substantive aspects of planning are the hardest to delimit: they can range into areas as divergent as housing, transportation, health services and economic development policy. Among major relevant substantive fields addressed in one planning theory text are urban growth, neighbourhood units, zoning, and the physical environment. Another anthology divides up the field by functional sectors: physical, social, public policy, and economic planning (Alexander 1992, p. 8).

Therefore, if we remain loyal to Banfield's already quoted formula, it is just the *relational process among different contents* and substantive aspects of planning that becomes the *substantive content of the planning theory*. Again, I agree with Alexander when he states:

> the core of planning theory is the planning process: how should and do people plan?";
> but, stating, at the same time, that "the planning theory explores the planning process and examines its components: What are they? How do they interrelate? How are they affected by the context of planning efforts? How do they determine planning outcomes? All these affect the question of how planning should be done (ibidem p. 9).

---

[21] The separation of "selection" from the "implementation" problem, has been one of the *leitmotifs* of the methodological reflections of a great planologist, Ragnar Frisch (see, 1970).

[22] See for instance the work of G. Benveniste (1987 and other works) and its reception in our community (the comments dedicated to him in issue No.8 of the journal *Planning Theory*). Frankly, I don't find anything new in this work compared to the past work of Banfield and Wilson (1963), Etzioni (1968), Rabinovitz (1967, 1969), Dennis (1970 and 1972), Dror (1971a and b) Robert Goodmann (1973); and in comparison to the simple, complete and elegant synthesis of the problem made by Faludi, in the last chapters of his first work (1973).

[23] The best synthesis of all the current strands of thought on planning theory is in Alexander's book (1992, second improved edition). Therefore, I have preferred to use that book for comments, even if other books have an equivalent validity in representing the current trend of thinking.

To me, all this constitutes a substantive theory or methodology of planning, approached from all sides.

1.4 Planning Theory: General or Not?

At one point (p. 10) Alexander states: "The eclectic nature of planning theory has so far resisted integration. There is no 'general theory of planning'; indeed, serious observers have expressed doubts whether the development of such a theory is even possible ...". In my opinion, it is not the eclectic nature of planning theory which has resisted integration, but only the eclectic nature of planning *tout court*.

Planning theory is either "*general*" or does not exist at all.

Planning theory (if a "rationale" has to exist and if it *can* exist) rests on the purpose of surpassing the eclectic nature of planning, in its substantive manifestations and applications; and providing to the different substantive planning methods a common field of understanding and consistency and (through understanding and consistency) a common process of decision and implementation.

Planning theory cannot split itself into different substantive forms or levels of planning; its role is to be a tool in monitoring consistency; and it has the synergetic role of facilitating implementation, when and where substantive planning fails because of its unilateral approach. That unilateral approach produces *bounded rationality* (in Simon's terms) or *sub-optimality* (in Pareto's terms), all this according to the unavoidable search for a higher "rationality".

In sum, without a search for a *general planning theory*, even a search for a planning theory *tout court* would not make sense. (Ragnar Frisch would call it "half logic"; and Dudley Seers "pseudo-planning")[24].

If we firmly anchor ourselves to Banfield's formula, the substance itself of planning theory is to elaborate a *general methodology of planning activities* and establish an operational nexus (*substantial* and *procedural* at the same time) among the different types of planning. Otherwise, we can remain too at-ease in our traditional substantive multiple cultures and practices of planning, without inventing our fantasy "stories" as "planning theory". In this case, I do not understand what this word "theory" has to do with those stories.

A similarly dangerous trend is the opposite belief that planning theory must be bound to some "theory of society". John Dyckman (1969, see also: 1966 and 1970) once said: "The theory of planning must include some theory of the society in which planning is institutionalised".

"*Must include?*" I agree, of course, with the remark that any planning activity can be strongly conditioned by the theory of society and also by institutions prevailing in the environment (in the country or any other form of community). Planning theory, however, must study a methodology of planning that does not recognise, per se, the peculiar conditions of each environment, and represents only a betterment of any

---

[24] Frisch 1970, 1976; Seers 1972.

practical mode of government and decision-making. So, it seems to me exactly that it *should not* "include" a theory of society.

The further adaptation of the methodology to individual circumstances is a successive skill, which has nothing to do with the foundations of the methods themselves. I cannot imagine the possibility of developing as many theories of planning as there may be theories of society that we can encounter or develop for each circumstance (country, community, form of government, and so on). Any discussion on the different theories of society would implicate a wide debate, and would transform planning theory (every man for himself!) into a sociological debate.

1.5 A Vade-Mecum for Good Planners' Professional Relations?

Many planning theorists think and argue that planning theory is justified because, for the practical professional planner (mainly the urban-planner), more than techniques, called "routine techniques," we need to understand:

> the planning process and the diverse roles in it of planners, their clients government, organizations, and institutions, and their members: elected and appointed officials, administrators, and other experts, and the public at large and its components: community elites and workers, suburbanites and central-city poor, organized interest groups and the "silent majority", "averages", and "minorities": women, blacks and other groups, handicapped, and elderly, and the young (Alexander 1986, Chap. 1).

But is it wise to consider all this as "the field of planning theory?" If that were the case, I would really be scared.

Without a doubt, all those things (along with many others) must be faced by the planner in the practical exercise of his or her profession. Without a doubt, he or she must be concerned about effective situations concerning the social and political environment in which he or she operates, as much as they are concerned about the physical or natural environment. But all this belongs to an obvious awareness which accompanies any kind of professional activity, more or less linked to social life (medicine, psychology, law, management, social defence and welfare, and, last but not least, political science). Besides, is that truly the "field" of the theory of (urban) planning? Or, rather, is it not the obvious context in which every professional can find himself operating? Analogously, could not the field, in the same way, of a "theory of medicine", or of a "theory of psychology", or of a "theory of law", or of a "theory of management sciences", or of a "theory of political science", and so on?

If the theory of planning should teach the planner to attend to all those things, it would represent a window on a very dangerous "holism"; a holism that has induced our planning theory literature to rush to busy itself with everything, to wear the shoes of others: the political scientist, the economist, the public manager, the jurist and the historian, or simply of the scholar of the most curious aspects of social history, (among dozens of cases, for instance, there is the history of Blues Heritage Conservation or of the Gay and Lesbian Emancipation[25]).

---

[25] See Clyde Woods' very interesting paper on *Blues Epistemology and Regional Planning History* (the case of the Lower Mississippi Delta Development Commission); Moira Kenney's

If the theory of planning has to find its own field, it seems to me convenient that it shall find it within the peculiarities of planning itself, that it shall provide a sort of reflection on itself, and, overall, shall provide a guarantee of consistency among multiple manifestations of planning and the substantive fields in which it operates (land use, economic and social investments, transport, environmental protection, health protection, and so on). We are always dealing with the consistency within a process which keeps its own identity: planning; and planning only.

This process needs to follow clear methods and procedures. It is not "routine", but a skill or "science", and we are dealing not with the political "feasibility" of the plans (which is a matter for the political scientist or the policy-maker), but with their "technical" feasibility (or "planological" feasibility).

In other words, planning theory must help planning to be really comprehensive and consistent; and I would like to consider this a "technical" aspect, the most important aspect of the true skill or professionalism of the planner. It is mainly through this kind of consistency and through the capacity of internal co-ordination, that plans achieve the condition to be politically implemented: not a sufficient condition, I agree, but an indispensable one.

If they become, further, politically implemented or not due to other historical or situational factors. For instance:

- the great power of subjects that operate for their own special interests and to damage the interests of others or the public interest;
- the interest of bureaucracy to hide its own administrative incapacity or interest;
- corruption, mafia or lobbying influencing the decision-making; and so on,

then the planner can take account of this only if it enters into an official and formal planning process, becoming the explicit objectives of the plans. But it seems to me that, to pay attention to those factors should not become the task of the planner (nor become, therefore, a "field" of planning theory) if we want to avoid the transformation of this theory into a permanent "tale" of particular situations, useless for all other particular situations[26].

It does not seem to me (even in the case of a systematic presence of the above factors) that we must include them in our planning "models", just to make the plans more "realistic" and probably more implementable. At most, we can agree to include, in the defined standard of a methodology of comprehensive planning, special moments of serious and engaging controls on the possible behaviour of groups or interests. We should pay attention to, as exogenous to the planning process, a grouped voicing of official stakeholders (through unobstructed enquiries or polls). This attention could belong to the field of planning theory (or methodology, in the sense I prefer to give to the word "theory"[27]). But it should be contained within the limits of a general list of

---

equally fascinating invitation to understand the *Urban aspects of Gay and Lesbian Marginalisation*. Both papers have been published in our journal *Planning Theory* (No. 13, 1995).

[26] For other points of view, see also Throgmorton, 1993 and 1996.

[27] According to the Oxford Dictionary, the word "theory" can have many meanings. Among them there are two distinct versions that can create some confusion in our use of the word:

prescriptions, operations to carry out in the preparations of plans and in their evaluation; not much more, otherwise planning theory (or methodology) risks transforming itself into a treatise of sociology, without the necessary competence and systematic consciousness.

1.6 Deontology and Epistemology of the Profession

Recently the planners' community, particularly that (still badly defined) of the *planning theorists*, has been stimulated to pay attention to the "ethical" aspects of the profession. However, a dichotomy between ethical approaches and epistemological approaches of planning has been proposed which, to me, does not seem to be correct.

In a book which people rightly considered as an occasion to pay attention to the ethical aspects of profession, and which includes the papers collected by Hu Thomas and Patsy Healey on the "Dilemmas of Planning Practice", the key concept of "validation of knowledge" is introduced (even in the subtitle of the book)[28]. In the preface the editors assert:

> Validation (of knowledge) did not seem to be an issue troubling our planners very greatly. This could either be because they have confidence in their basic knowledge; or, it could be because British planners have long ceased to worry about having a knowledge-base and are far more concerned about being able to operate effectively. "How do I do …?" has replaced, "What do I know? as the question which excites (or worries) planners (Thomas and Healey 1991).

I would like to think that this remark fits well with my remark concerning the dangerous trend taken in planning theory: in essence that there is too much room for "how do we do" problems and too little room for "what do we know" problems. I would like to add more room for the problem, "what do we know about our needed know-how". This last question should become, in my opinion, the core of the next planning theory.

Of course, this is an *epistemological* approach. But it is, at the same time, a *deontological* problem, i.e., a problem of professional ethics. Many other important ethical problems (I prefer to call them "value" problems) concern planners, along with the other members of any community. But we must not confuse the (epistemological or deontological) problems of planners with any other social and community problems concerning the entire society and the kind of constitution it prefers or achieves. If, personally, I am persuaded that there does not generally exist any kind of scientific progress (advancement or findings) that is totally independent from historico-social, institutional, and even "partisan" values or interests, it still seems to me very important to keep a *technical* approach to our professional role, as in the educational role,

---

1. "a supposition or system of ideas explaining something, esp. one based on general principles independent of the particular things to be explained (atomic theory, theory of evolution)"; 2. "the exposition of the principles of a science, etc. (the theory of music)". It is self-evident that my preferred meaning is this last (even because it is the most used, in the continental use: French, German, Italian); whilst in the English tradition, perhaps, the first is more familiar.

[28] Thomas and Healey, *Dilemma of Planning Practice*, 1991.

just to safeguard intellectual honesty and the respect of true and free opinions, and to realise a superior capacity to achieve results from a general point of view[29].

And the first thing that needs to be "generalised" is the *planning know-how*, i.e., planning theory.

To confuse planning theory with any other sort of social theory risks *de-professionalizing* planning. It means to forsake and discredit planning as a profession, and to intone (maybe even with charming and delightful songs) its requiem.

---

[29] This is the way I interprete the interesting argument by Luigi Mazza (1995) and Dan Alexander Seni (1996a and b).

2

In Search of Integration: The Past Negative Experience

2.1 Expectations and Results from the Integration of the Planning Sciences

From what has been said in the last chapter, does there emerge any kind of chance to reconstruct the basic field of a planning theory? Is there a definable field for planning theory?

I resume again my critical thesis. This thesis is that, instead of developing truly interdisciplinary approaches and producing new learning bases for the preparation of plans (in a context which would be in support of a *planning society*, to again use Faludi's nice expression[1]) in the name of planning theory, a sort of planning "self-analysis" or "meta-analysis" has broken out. This type of analysis has led to the crumbling of everything that could be consolidated and cohesive in planning, through its methods and practices.

People should expect a broadening, a unification, and an integration of the different approaches and fields of planning, at least those practised for public purposes (from physical-spatial to economic and social)[2]. Instead, what we have achieved is a more brooding procedure, approach by approach, field by field, which has led to a sort of solipsism within each conventional discipline (economists with economists, town planners with town planners, systems analysts and engineers with systems analysts and engineers, social planners with social planners, etc.). Within each of these groups, it is surprising how little acquaintance there is with the most important theoretical contributions developed by the others.

Just to cite one glaring example: how familiar are the planning theorists who come from the conventional town planning point of view with the work of the planning theorists who come from the economic point of view, such as Frisch, Tinbergen (both Nobel Prize winners), Leif Johansen and many others?

---

[1] See, of course, Faludi (1973): the last chapter.

[2] On this point see the contents of integration outlined in my previously quoted paper prepared for the "First World-wide Conference on Planning Sciences" (Archibugi 1996), but also my obstinate research from the past (1969, 1974, 1989).

And, in reverse, how familiar are those theorists coming from the economic point of view with the important contributions made to planning theory by town planners of quality, such as Doxiades, Chapin, Perloff, and many others? With the last generous effort by John Friedmann (1987), one of the "planning theorists" most engaged in an integrative approach[3], we can go to the origins, or roots, of the historical disciplines, in order to find a significant common field of analysis and to synthesise an interdisciplinary approach.

But a reconstruction aimed at an evaluation of the present status of comprehensive planning doesn't exist in the literature. The important work of Nathaniel Lichfield (1996), which summarizes his many years of professional experience, covers this lack. It concerns, however, mainly the field of economic evaluation of plans, and less the inter-relationship of plans among different levels and scales.

I will give some examples which I hope will be familiar to everyone (at least as historical events).

2.1.1 Macro-Economic Planning in Europe

When, during the 1960s, in several countries of Western Europe, people tried to introduce (with stronger ideological resistance) the methods and procedures of macro-economic governance known as *economic programming*, (with the French *Commissariat au Plan*'s multi-year plans, the "Naddy" in Great Britain, the experiments with economic programming in Italy and Spain, and the even more advanced methods developed in the Netherlands, Norway, Belgium, Denmark, others countries, and even at the European Community scale[4]) many regretted that this sort of planning did not take into account any social, urban, or operational features.

Many trials were developed that tried to integrate macro-economic planning and physical planning at the national scale. The most obvious bridge between these two kinds of planning has been the regional splitting of national plans (called "*regional policies*" in many countries). This was also the epoch when, to use an expression used by Alonso (1971) in a paper dealing with the integration problem, the "regional science" as a "meta-discipline" was born[5].

In the USA, a country with a demographic and territorial size not comparable to European countries, this integrative role has been played by *state planning*.

An example of an attempt to integrate macro-economic programming or planning with regional and spatial planning that I know better, of course, is the Italian "*Progetto 80*". But other attempts have been developed in the Netherlands, in France, and (in the 1970s) in Germany, with the Federal "*Raumordnungsprogramme*", that has since been put aside.

---

[3] I would draw your attention to one of Friedman's papers (1973).

[4] For a rapid appraisal of these experiences as a whole, see a paper of Albrechts (1992).

[5] The title of his paper (presented in Japan in an academic meeting of "regional sciences") was "*Beyond Interdisciplinary Approach to Planning*" (1971).

But the cases of real operational integration have remained very rare, as a consequence of the lack of a real disciplinary integration[6].

2.1.2 Strategic Management and Planning in the Public Sector

When, in the 1960s, strategic management and planning was developed in business corporations and even in governmental agencies (local, state, and federal) through the impulse of systems analysis, engineering, and operational research, various attempts were implemented to *integrate* the methods of macro-economic planning with (at least) public expenditure and budgeting practices. It is well known that attempts were made to introduce such methods into many governmental agencies. Other efforts have been made to integrate the methods at the local governmental scale.

This is the case of the experimental analysis by the British IOR Group (Institute of Operational Research), which was very influential at that time on Faludi's methodological reflections, and must be considered a good test of the benefits of an interdisciplinary consciousness (Friend and Jessop 1969, 1974).

Furthermore, there are the well-known attempts to introduce the PPBS (Planning-Programming-Budgeting-System) and similar procedures for evaluation in the US Federal and local administrations, and the RCB (*Rationalisation des Choix Budgétaires*) in France. All these attempts failed, in my opinion because of the lack of connections to macro-economic planning (and even with a mere budgetary policy at the national scale, which was also lacking).

2.1.3 Integrated Regional Planning

When, in the 1970s, some governments tried to take a more generalised approach to urban planning (which traditionally had been physical in orientation, and until that moment carried out in isolation and limited to land-use aspects), many attempts were made to go beyond this character and to integrate physical and industrial planning at the regional and local scale (for example the *structure plans* carried out by counties in England). With respect to this experience, I conjecture that the difficulties met by the "structure plans" in becoming a stable operating system are due to the fact that they were not framed in a national, multi-county scenario, capable of controlling the consistency between county design and national decisions and design.

2.1.4 Integrated Approach in Academic Journals

We could continue with many other cases of attempts to *integrate* different typologies and scales of planning that have been researched, but not (yet) achieved.

Two academic journals born in the 1960s, *Socio-Economic Planning Sciences* published by Pergamon and *Environment and Planning* published by Pion, were aimed at

---

[6] Some critical surveys of these experiences in Europe are in a book by Stuart Holland, ed., (entitled: *"Beyond Capitalistic Planning"*, Oxford, 1978). For the US experience, see an enlightening essay by Beauregard (1992) for the "First World Conference on Planning Science" (Palermo 1992).

the fostering of an academic integration of planning theory. The first included, on its editorial board, economists of the level of Ragnar Frisch and H. Darin-Drabkin, town planners such as Britton Harris, Martin Meyerson and John Dyckman, and system analysts such as R.H. Howard and H.G. Berkman. The second had economists such as Peter Nijkamp, town planners such as Peter Hall, system analysts such as R. Quandt, etc.) But, the expectations in this direction were largely frustrated. These journals have developed their own "core focuses": *Socio-Economic Planning Sciences* deals mainly with conventional "operational research" disciplines (even if applied to the public and social sectors), and *Environment and Planning* covers conventional "regional science" with a strong orientation towards a positive, neo-classical, economic approach and therefore with scarce interest in planning (until more recent years, when it has been extended with other subjects and with the publication of new accompanying journals).

I believe that this has happened, not due to the responsibility of the editors (or their respective editorial boards, of which, incidentally, I have been a member since their inceptions), but due to a lack, within the academic and professional worlds, of a real tendency towards important integrated experiences in planning.

I have evoked these cases only as well-known examples which support my reasoning. Each of them, of course, deserves a more systematic and careful illustration, whilst very few remain in our memory, and absolutely none in the memory of some of our younger colleagues[7].

In conclusion (to return to the thread of my initial reasoning), people should expect progress *towards an ever deeper refinement and methodological integration of different kinds of planning* (in order to strengthen a general methodology of planning) which in turn could strengthen at the same time:

a. techniques and capacity for analysis of the discipline itself; and
b. the applied results of the discipline, by which I mean the *plans* and their capacity to be implemented with a more comprehensive outcome that is more consistent with the conditions and constraints of their environment in a programming vision, rendering them more feasible.

It is in this direction that one could expect the emerging "planning theory" to lead us, and it is in this progressive direction that Faludi's expression of the theory *of* planning deserves to go.

---

[7] I have produced a critical survey of the more meaningful research strands which have contributed, consciously or not, to the realisation of a certain *integration*, either disciplinary or operative, of various *fields* and *approaches* of planning. The purpose would be to set the foundations of a new "science" or "theory" of planning. I have called this work, on which I have been working for some years, *Introduction to Planology*. To me, these words seem useful in indicating this attempt to unify, within a general historical-cultural perspective, all of the sectorial approaches belonging to the planning sciences in the last decades, and to examine their connections and the convergence towards a new unique discipline. There is a draft version of this survey, published by the Planning Studies Centre (Archibugi 1992) but I hope to soon conclude a new completed version of that essay.

2.2 The Bad Course of the Debate

Things however did not run along this road. On the contrary (and this I say with much regret), a different road has been taken, one that contains a continuous flow of consideration *of* and reflections *about* planning (does this deserve the name, *theory?*). This road leads towards a great noisy chattering about planning, its institutional constraints, its *bounded rationality*, etc. which has been dignified by someone as *post-modern*.

A lot of insights have been developed; sometimes (but not always) even interesting ones, influenced by a kind of psychology and polity of behaviour by individuals, groups, communities, and institutions. I call this a sort of *politology of planning*, based essentially on the willingness of the people (and generally the *lack of willingness* of these people). This is called *realism*. I resist, out of respect for the earlier efforts of Faludi and some others, calling this a *theory of planning*.

Some of these considerations and reflections are based on the ingenuous background of a reduced version of utilitarian-type philosophy. Or, they are based on philosophies that are poorly and only intuitively assimilated. People have shown a preferred tendency to develop a sort of philosophy of incapacity: incapacity to implement plans, incapacity to apply appropriate future projections, incapacity to make rational decisions, incapacity to implement organisational schemes, and so on. All this is professed as if it were the outcome of a peculiar wisdom. I have the impression that from all this chattering (which we continue to call planning theory) we inadvertently are singing a sort of great requiem for planning[8].

If I decided, after years of indecision, to intervene in the debate about the theory *on* planning[9], (a meta-debate that I hope nobody would get the idea to call pompously *the theory of planning theory*), it is because I feel a danger from this to the profession and for planning activities in general; and I feel the need to invite my colleagues to cut this useless waste of intellectual (and sometimes even sophisticated) resources, and to approach students through a learning process involving *know-how*, *methods*, and, if well framed within the methods, *techniques*, so scarcely acquired in the past, and so important for the improvement of the implementation of plans. Further, I feel the need that *planning theory* be restored to its original role of dealing with the logical and operational frame of *any* planning approach or planning activity.

Planning theory would work much better in the neglected direction of the *integration of the approaches* (trying to bring into the discussion many types of scholars involved in many different types of planning, which presently is not the case). In

---

[8] Even the arguments of this chapter, I agree, belong to this kind of literature. I must confess that I am writing it with a certain uneasiness. In brief, I would prefer to occupy myself (and it is what I have tried to do to a certain extent in proposing something different) didactically and in scholarly terms, on *how to prepare* and *how to manage* a plan, in terms of consistency and relationship with the outer environment, instead of engaging in meta-talks *on* plans.

[9] I felt that the 1998 Oxford conference (where I presented the core of the arguments of this chapter) was the appropriate place to do that.

searching for such an integration of approaches, planning theory could discuss *how to make connections*, logical and methodological, among the different *scales* of planning (suburban, urban, metropolitan, regional, national, international, global), among the different *sectors* of planning (agricultural, industrial, commercial, services, governmental), and among the different *units* of planning (communities, unions, associations, "stakeholders," political institutions)[10].

A *planning society*, especially in a pluralist society or world, cannot avoid defining the machinery through which each unit, scale, or sector makes its own planning activities consistent with the planning activities of *others*, within a less casual and disordered frame than in a non-planning society. This *non-planning society* is the object, *against* which planning activities, the planning profession, planning schools, and therefore planning theory, should be erected.

And this definition of the planning society and its operative functioning should be the appropriate *field* of planning theory.

It is obvious that this "rational" vision of the planning system (and how could it be otherwise?) is an abstract picture that could be founded only with difficulty in the (ex-post) reality. From time immemorial, however, planning has taken this for granted (and to return to it seems to me useless). Inherent in the concept of planning is the recognition that an ideal is not a fixed objective, but itself will change. The rational plan *"can be striven for, but never achieved"*[11].

This fact does not negate the usefulness and effectiveness of rational planning. On the contrary, it constitutes its rationale, or *raison d'etre*, and this is a point which we should avoid questioning (at least after Condorcet) when we look at the not-always-rational nor enlightened progress of humankind.

2.3 Is a Positive Reconstruction of Planning Theory Possible?

To make a positive contribution to the restoration of a more useful and constructive theory *of* planning, of the kind above outlined, I will sketch out (only in a impressionistic way) which of the ambits or fields of research such a theory of planning, in my opinion, should advance.

As I have said, it is a matter of determining which research fields could contribute to the *integration* of different approaches to planning, to the unification of some cognitive and analytical tools, to the development of a common language, and even *lexicon*, (an aspect that planning theory has also neglected), and to the co-ordination of a *tax-*

---

[10] This is what I will do, in a preliminary way, in Chap. 6.

[11] This is how the idea of the planning activity was presented by a MIT professor, John T. Howard in the entry for *City Planning* in the Encyclopaedia Britannica in the 1930s. This quotation is taken from a work of mine on the *Theory of Urbanistics* (forthcoming in English).

onomy among different plans and planning activities. All this, in my view, should be the privileged task of a renovated *theory of planning*[12].

This also would be the way to resuscitate planning from the loquacious catalepsy into which it seems to have fallen.

---

[12] At the moment, the most useful material for the construction (or re-construction) of this "building" joint venture are some epistemological writings, outsider (!) the narrow networking debate *on* planning theory. Examples? 1) The W. Yeechong's (1984) exhaustive and accurate essay on a "hermeneutical theory of planning build on the ideas of Habermas and Gadamer"; 2) the William Salet's (1982, already quoted) paper about the 'quest for identity' concerning planning theory; 3) the Farago's essay (2004) on a "general theory for public (spatial) planning". About this last essay I am very grateful to Andreas Faludi to having informed me and attired my attention on this work, besides in consideration that Faludi himself is the scholar who has traced – some time ago, at least in the urban planning *milieu* – the guideline for a work of this kind (see Faludi, 1971). Anyhow it is possible that many other colleagues have worked in this direction and could cooperate in the purposeful reconstruction (see Benli's consideration on the current state of planning, 2004)). Other supports to an idea of reconstruction of a true theory of planning are in same dispersed past writings of authors placed apparently a little outside the planning theory debate which I consider worthy to be not forgotten. Among them Marc Los (already quoted) (1981, Rein Scheele (1982), Kraushaar & Gardels (1982) and Jenny Poxon (1998).

3

Towards a New Unified Discipline of Planning

3.1 The Fields of Activity

In Chap. 2, I made reference to several research fields, and various disciplinary domains and historical-cultural roots, in order to reconstruct in an integrative way the theory of planning.

The fields of research and activity alluded to are those in which planning has, with varying degrees of success, been applied. These fields are many, but in attempting to summarise (not without the risk of over-simplification and unjust omissions), I have gathered them into the following (ordered not according to importance but to their historical occurrence): (a) physical planning, i.e., urban and territorial; (b) (macro-) economic planning, (c) social planning; (d) development planning; and (e) operational planning. Allow me to summarise, hurriedly and therefore perhaps disrespectfully, the nature and confines of these five fields.

3.1.1 Physical Planning

Physical planning was the first (I think) to be born as a field of activity: it arose from the need to plan the physical development of the cities.

Although many place its origins in the utopian designs of "cities of the future" (designs that have always existed and flourished particularly around the turn of the 18th century), it appears historically as an extension of the "art" of building construction. It is no coincidence that the first texts on urban planning went under the name of "the art of building the city"[1]. It's hard to imagine other reasons for which urban planning (as a discipline of study and professional training) developed in the early decades of the last century as an off-shoot of architecture.

---

[1] Keep in mind the first handbooks of town-planning in Germany: by Reinhard Baumeister (*The Enlargement of Cities in its Technical, Building Policy, and Economic Aspects*, 1876) and by Joseph Stübben (*The Building of the City*, 1890), and something of this kind would have been proposed by the so-called "urbanistic" popes of the 15th and 16th centuries, had they theorised their interventions on Rome.

Despite planning, right from the beginning of that century, having been heavily influenced by organic theories (like those of Patrick Geddes, who was a biologist by training and culture), in actual fact "master plans" or "plans directeurs" are still essentially, for better or worse, plans for the physical construction of cities. The rest is academic.

In time, physical planning became extended to include non-urban areas, with the intention of viewing the development of town and countryside as a whole. In more recent times, in fact very recently, this planning area has spread to include the "environment" in general (meaning the physical environment, however), giving rise to what is often called "environmental planning".

One cannot forget that, in recent times, there has developed from planning culture and in particular, from that of the Anglo-Saxon tradition, a special area of reflection amongst planners called "planning theory". This represents one of the "critical points" in the conceptual renewal of planning itself.

It is remarkable (but also symptomatic) that, apart from a few rare cases, planning theory development has not gone beyond the ambit of physical planning, even though it could well have been of interest to other fields of planning (about which we will speak shortly). The best known exponent of this strand is Faludi, the author of an initial *summa* of Planning Theory, with which the strand began (Faludi 1973). In the last two decades the debate has been greatly extended. An intelligent, instructive summary can be found in Alexander (1986).

3.1.2 Macro-Economic Planning

The other activity field in which planning has had an important and "classical" role is that of economic planning.

Its operational scale has been (and still is) that of national governmental communities (where it is takes the form of macro-economic planning).

Economic planning has been applied largely at the scale of minor operational and productive unities (firms, especially big business). In these cases, even if it has adopted techniques similar to those at the national scale, it has faced problems and consequently developed methods so different that it is impossible to consider large- and small-scale economic planning in the same group. We will talk about small-scale economic planning below with the title of "operational planning" (even if it is essentially of the economic type).

Returning now to large-scale economic planning, its first application found maturity during the First World War with the need to manage resources, rationally and strategically, in a time of great scarcity[2].

---

[2] From positions of responsibility assumed during the war, Herbert Hoover (in the USA) and Walter Rathenau (in Germany) introduced planning methods for the management of war materials and national resources in general, which may be considered the forerunners of economic planning. Probably also in other countries, the phenomena of the "war economy" has been registered that have given rise to forms of planning (which now escape attention); a work rich in information on this topic is the book of Thomas Wilson (1964).

But it is in the context of the Soviet communist regime that economic planning had its first well-known and debated manifestations. As it was inserted in an institutional context, based on the principles of collective ownership of the means of production (even the land), Soviet economic planning was soon identified with the political regime under which it was applied. This left little room for sophisticated conceptual distinctions in the West, and has represented a formidable weapon for those opposed to the introduction of economic planning in the West, who have benefited for the last 70 years from the political horror to which this regime gave rise, in order to discredit the instruments as well as the politics that were practised in the USSR. Even today there are many who are disposed to argue that the collapse of the regime was due to economic planning rather than the political regime which applied it, thus ignoring the incredible progress made in the USSR at the technological as well as economic level with respect to its starting point. This happened thanks to complex management of the economy and in spite of errors made in the final choices of allocation of resources which the regime imposed on its own planning process.

In spite of this, the idea of a more rational management of capitalist or market economies (underlining the structural differences between the economic "systems" referred to) has encouraged the development in the post war period of more systematic political economic interventions on the part of various national governments, by means of the progressive and experimental introduction of systems of central planning.

France and Japan were the first to officially instigate economic planning processes, the former with the *Commissariat au Plan*, the latter with the "Agency for Economic Planning". Claiming to be distinct from the Soviet experience, their activity was named "indicative" planning. Many countries followed suit[3]: the Netherlands, Norway, and in the 1960s Belgium, Great Britain, Italy and Denmark. All these began to experiment with "indicative" planning, as opposed to that practiced in "collectivist" economy regimes (which was called "imperative" planning). It was also necessary to overcome the opposition of a well-rooted *laissez faire* culture.

Even in the USA (where indicative planning experiments resulted in the National Planning Board of 1934), during the late post-war period, despite the unfavourable climate resulting from the growing threat of Stalinist imperialism and from the need to not risk compromise with that which revealed itself as the enemy of "free enterprise", there was the expansion of indicative planning experiences at the level of economically depressed regions, at State level and finally at a federal level, with the reiterated appeal

---

It is with melancholy, and partly with rage, that I must acknowledge that the birth of the attention to the "strategic use" of national resources, and therefore, the assessment of forms of planning at national scale, with the derivative techniques and methods, should be owed to the necessity of the conditions of warfare. I would be much happier, today, if it could be more usual to talk about a "war against underdevelopment," or a "war against poverty," or a "war against environmental and natural degradation," and so on.

[3] This refers particularly to the French experience since that of Japan, though perhaps historically more effective, remained alien to Europeans. This may be due to linguistic and cultural barriers as well as incomparable socio-economic structures.

for the definition of "national objectives"[4] of public expenditure, particularly federal (with the application of PPBS methods, already mentioned, and on which will follow more arguments below).

Macro-economic planning has naturally leant on the theorems of macro-economics (the theory of general equilibrium and Keynesian theory), in that it applies itself to a system of quantifiable variables of the socio-economic phenomena that need to be managed (income and its distribution, employment, productivity, foreign trade accounts, public debt, consumption, investments, etc.), and in that it utilises criteria and techniques used in operational research in order to introduce optimal choices (i.e., constrained maximum) in economic policy. It was Jan Tinbergen and his school that codified planning procedures, or quantitative theory, in economic policy. Such experiences have, however, matured in various centres of thought and application, linked to central planning offices including that of the USSR[5].

3.1.3 Social Planning

Social planning represents a field of activities consisting of components that are not always assimilable into a unitary whole.

This field of planning was born and developed above all at the local and community level with small projects, and is pervaded throughout its development by an anti-centralist and localist rhetoric. It covers a vast field of action (education, health, social integration, living and working conditions, women, children, the elderly, crime, etc.) and thus, by its very nature, leads to a particular openness with regard to "integration" of approaches. It is pervaded by an almost religious faith in the efficacy of "planning from the bottom". It extols voluntary action and participation.

This kind of planning has found its operational stimuli in all situations and it is present in all historical experiences. It is the field of social planning that is least contested and least obstructed; this is partly because its fragmentation and relative unsystematicness keep it far from the research and respect of "rational" paradigms. This has rendered it somewhat spurious to the strictly defined fields of planning. The most extensive and forceful manifestation of social planning has taken place in those coun-

---

[4] The swan-song of macro-economics in the USA has been the report of a special advisory committee on the "national growth policy processes" created within the National Commission on supplies and shortage (a joint commission President-Congress basically bi-partisan) in 1976, not by chance created under the pressure of the scarcity of energy resources, and other shortages, provoked by the Yom Kippur War. The report gave motivations and modality for the introduction of economic planning processes at federal scale (US Advisory Committee etc. 1977).

[5] Until the sixties, the Kantorovich school pressed for the introduction of "optimal planning" in Gosplan methods, but with little political success (see the English translation of a work of 1959). On macro-economic planning as a whole I could not do better than recommend the last work, which is unfortunately not very well known, of Leif Johansen (1977) in two volumes, (the third was halted by his death). Obviously one cannot but recommend the notes and fundamental contribution of Jan Tinbergen (1952, 1956, 1964), and also Ragnar Frisch's last essays (published posthumously 1976).

tries where the "welfare state" has been most effective and where there has been more public spending in this sector, favouring the creation of an army of social workers.

The merits of social planning are numerous. I will give an incomplete summary of them:

- in the first place, the merit of having arrogated for itself the unilaterality of the "economic" approach (with its strongly limited "rationality");
- in the second place that of having always criticised the significance of (macro)economic aggregation and the capacity of the latter's variables in determining objective-functions, or "collective preferences" in economic planning processes;
- thirdly, it has stressed the participative aspects and thus also those related to negotiation in all planning processes;
- fourthly, the merit of having extended the spirit (through all its micro-projects) of "evaluation" of results, this has contributed greatly to the "rationalisation" of all planning projects and has helped give "evaluation" its proper place in planning even outside the field of social planning; and
- in the fifth place, it has opened the doors to a wider concept of "development planning" through its sensitivity to problems which are not strictly speaking economic, but rather socio cultural;
- finally, and this sums up the above, social planning has constituted the most important base for the launch of an integrated or unified approach to planning from the technical as well as the political point of view[6].

3.1.4 Development Planning

This planning field of developmental activity can be considered special in that the implementation of plans is assessed not for its performance per se, but rather for the quality of the terrain on which these activities take place. The planning field to which I refer consists of the developing countries[7].

This field is divided into two distinct areas: development planning as it regards each developing area (whether country or region) and as it regards the planning relationship between developed and developing countries.

In both cases, the field and sub-fields have been and still are the object of direct interest on the part of the UN system, and it is in this ambit that they have developed.

However, in this field as well, there has been nothing but frustration.

As regards individual countries, the management of development that should have been the object of "planning" has suffered a fate resulting from the political instability often found in these countries, from their political and economic dependence, from

---

[6] This approach was never really applied, though it was strongly desired and projected by the UN: Resolutions 1139/1966; 1320/1968; 1491/1970 of ECOSOC, the Economic and Social Council of the UN; and, its last important manifestation, Resolution 2681/1970 of the General Assembly. It was an approach likewise promoted by official UN research institutions (UNRISD, 1975 and 1980).

[7] This does not change the fact that the term has often been applied to the development of "developed" countries. But in such cases the activity field loses its identity and becomes more similar to macro-economic planning.

their inability to integrate at a multi-national level (perhaps as a result of their political dependence mentioned above), and from a cultural precariousness that has put them in a position of not being able to rely on an effective administrative and operational structure that is easily adaptable to new methods. From a certain point of view, the absence of consolidated interests and of a pluralism of self-regulating economic activities could have placed the developing countries in a more favourable position regarding the introduction of rational methods that would have conflicted less than in the developed countries with constituted interests, privileges, and historically acquired customs. However, the absence proportionally of an evolved and aware ruling class more than compensated negatively for the absence of institutional obstacles put in the way of planning.

At the level of the overall relationship between North and South, despite laudable efforts on the part of the international agencies that have always been prompt to suggest supra-national methods of management and government, development planning has been frustrated by:

- the persistent resistance by the great powers to the strengthening of supra-national powers and the adoption of truly multilateral methods of cooperation for development;
- the great Western powers' interest in maintaining, for the purpose of commercial hegemony and political expediency, a relationship of bilateral dependency; the tendency of developing countries to compete amongst themselves and seek bilateral privileges wherever possible;
- internal conflict between the developing countries' autochthonous internal interests and powers, which is sometimes exploited by the developed countries and sometimes suffered passively for reasons of political opportunism; and, above all,
- the adaptation to a freer, more modern and internationalist expression of national policy in developed Western countries instead of the persistent fear of the cold war and that of an ever incumbent totalitarian regime on a world scale.

Despite all this, the UN has tried to introduce a world development observatory and to elaborate some unitary development planning policies. To these attempts must be ascribed the activities of the Committee for Development Planning headed by Jan Tinbergen (see Tinbergen 1966 and 1968), and the efforts to model world economic relations (directed by Wassily Leontief; (see Leontief 1974 and 1977): unfortunately these have not had the necessary political support and follow-up.

But one might also ask oneself whether there has been adequate support from the scientific community, and from all those informal non-governmental groupings that, together with the scientific community, have an important role in the promotion of concepts and initiatives.

Development planning, however, is a field in which various disciplines have met and collided, because in it (more than in other fields) there have been realised integrated forms of economic, social and even physical planning. The very "simple" nature of the economic structures involved (those of developing countries) also related it directly to individual "intervention projects". This opened the way to a further specific "field" of planning, that which we will call "operational" (of which more later), in which the "economic" discipline meets the engineering and managerial disciplines, and in which macro-economic planning comes widely into contact with microeconomic approaches (cost-benefit analysis).

3.1.5 Operational Planning

The field of operational planning therefore represents fertile ground for disciplinary integration, and although this field has had an important role in development planning (in the developing countries), it has been equally applied and developed in complex and advanced economies. Here, planning science has almost rediscovered its origins: as management science. We mean by the origins of planning, the first (to a greater or lesser extent utopian) applications of engineering to social projects and to any form of public administration[8].

Operational planning is also composed of two areas (which are somewhat distinct in practice, but difficult to distinguish in theory): (a) the planning of single "projects" which we can call "micro-operational"; and (b) the planning of entire operational sectors of administration and public expenditure, which we can call "macro-operational".

Both areas of operational planning draw from the theoretical and practical experiences of "management", and the sciences that have formed themselves around it: valuation science, decision science, and planning science itself. By their very nature these do not take into consideration the public or private nature of the plans to which they are applied. Both operational planning areas draw on the progress made in applied mathematics (matrix-analysis, factors-analysis, multi-criteria analysis, game theory, etc.), and in operational research (linear-, non-linear-, quadratic-, dynamic-programming etc.) in the introduction of typically trans-disciplinary tools of analysis and evaluation (of which more later).

Micro-operational planning, even if applied to public projects, applies to the variables (and also the theorems) of micro-economics, and its accounting system, which, in the institutional development of modern market economics, is the economy of individual, usually private concern. It is founded on the concept of the "project" (whether public or private) and on its evaluation[9].

---

[8] Let us not forget that the first educational sanctuary of the social planners was the French "Ecole Politechnique" (later copied in other states), from which a number of reformers emerged, including Saint-Simon, Comte, Considerant and others. Nor should we forget that the first attempts at large scale economic planning were considered questions of management of scarce resources (primary resources and foodstuffs) during the First World War (as mentioned above) and that these were carried out by polytechnic engineers more or less introduced to management of industrial firms (the already mentioned Walter Rathenau in Germany, graduate of the Polytechnic of Karlsruhe, Herbert C. Hoover in the USA, engineering graduate of Stanford). In the USSR, Lenin saw planning as a grand enterprise of engineering management at the scale of the entire economy, influenced by his fascination for capitalist industrial management (much as Marx was fascinated by entrepreneurship in his time).

[9] In the form concerned with the management of enterprise, especially in the case of large firms, operational planning becomes "corporate planning". This constitutes another great

On the other hand macro-operational planning, which is essentially public in character, applies to the variables and theorems of macro-economics, and its accounting system[10].

Operational planning, both in its micro version (corporate and project) and its macro version (programmes and public expenditure), has two fundamental evaluative approaches which are both practiced and both justified. The first is that which concerns the management of the concern or the project per se (time, efficiency, minimalisation of costs and maximisation of returns) and which we could define as "internal" evaluation. The second concerns the relationship and the impact of the undertaking, project or programme *as it regards its surroundings*, (compatibility and coordination with other projects, positive or negative effects on the economic system in general, on the physical environment, on social conditions, conformity with and level of achievement of goals etc.); this second approach could be defined as "external" evaluation. Using a language that has become current, we can say that the first is aimed at the *efficiency* of the projects, and the second at their effectiveness.

Operational planning, in both versions, has meant an integration of approaches between the economic and engineering disciplines and, more recently, between those of systems engineering, operational research, praxeology[11], and management science[12].

These approaches have constituted the direct premises for the consideration of the systemic relations between micro and macro programming and between the internal evaluation approach and the external one. This greater attention given to systemic relations has constituted, therefore, the basis for the framework of operational planning: at the level of single "planning units" (where it was born) out of the logic of "projects"; and in the vaster and more complex planning whole in the logic of "programmes" and "plans".

---

field of planning, which has not been discussed so far since it lies outside the horizons of our concerns: planning in the public and community interest.

[10] Macro-economic planning (mentioned in Sect. 1.2) has employed products of operational planning to a large extent, applying these at the macro-economic level (arguably the work of Tinbergen and his school can be interpreted in this way). It seems that, for the second time in its history, economics is a tributary of corporate theory. Just as the old political economics was born as a generalisation of the micro-economic theory of the firm, the "new" economic policy, which is essentially macro-economic planning, can be seen as a generalisation of operational planning of large scale industry. The description of the nation in terms of one "great firm", so dear to Leninists and socialists, has now even become part of the language of journalists.

[11] As it has been called by Kotarbinski (1965) and others.

[12] If asked to present notable examples of this approach we should recall the works of Simon (from the first in 1947 to those of 1957 and 1969); Churchmann (see for example his works of 1961 and 1968); Ozbekhan (see first and foremost his general report to a meeting of the OECD in 1969), and Ackoff (1962 and 1974). As for expressions directed at the integration of economics and operational research, apart from the works of Kantorovich (1959) and his school, and of Dantzig (1957), I have in mind a work by Bellman (1957), the works of Dorfman et al (1958), and a volume by Baumol (1961), which are particularly representative of these approaches.

We may define this "framework," not as a rejection or critique of micro-projecting, but rather as the emergence of macro-planning as a prerequisite that gives micro-projecting (and operational planning, for which it acts as a vehicle) the guarantee of "optimal performance" and thus avoids the persistent risks of "sub-optimal performance".[13]

This has been not only the technical meeting point (operational analysis applied to macro-economic theorems), but also the "political" meeting point (programming of public expenditure) between operational planning and macro-economic planning (as planning fields of action). In the shape of the programming of public expenditure, it has generated "systems analysis" for the various public programmes. After having begun in the USA in the defence programme sector, it was then extended in the 1960s to the programmes of the Federal Department of Health, Education and Welfare and subsequently to all the Federal agencies, by means of the PPBS (the "Planning, Programming, Budgeting System"). It has constituted an important strand in planning activities.[14] It was extended to all levels of public spending and to many other countries, as we will see in Chap. 7.

This, too, has been obstructed in various ways by disciplinary schools and tendencies, not least in this case by that of "macro-economic planning". The systemic approach should have convinced everybody that the operational planning of public spending was not contradictory but rather complementary, when necessary, to macro-economic planning. Likewise it could be complementary to social planning (to which it is related) and also to physical planning.

Operational planning of public spending (or simply the programming of the same) has also become the ground on which various disciplines have met, and in part clashed: above all the administrative sciences, with their fund of "transdisciplinary" techniques deriving from systems engineering and operational research, have clashed with economic-political analysis. This meeting, which has been enriched (and in some ways contested) by the sociological analysis of the relationship between "public" or "social choice" and "individual" choice (about which a sophisticated debate has taken place which shows no signs of attenuating)[15], has resulted in a complex science, or theory: that of "political decision science or theory", or simply "policy science"[16].

---

[13] I have elaborated on these aspects in another work (Archibugi 1989).

[14] For a general overview, see the works of Schultze (1968 and 1970); the essays collected by Novick (1965) and those contained in a publication of the US Congress (1969) on the experience of the PPBS. For more theoretical aspects see McKean (1958 and 1968) and Olson (1973). There is a useful panorama in Haveman (1970).

[15] I refer to the debate concerning the possibility of social choice developed by "welfare-economics" economists; (the major exponent of which is Arrow with his fundamental text of 1951, and also his more recent work of 1986 in collaboration with H. Raynaud; also to be remembered is the work of A.K. Sen, 1970, 1982 and 1986). I refer also to the contribution given by "public choice" theory from "public economics" scholars (see as the major exponent Buchanan, 1962, with Tullock, and 1967). A vast review of the debate, complete with an exhaustive bibliography, is in Müller, 1989.

[16] See above all Dror (1968, 1971a and 1971b).

3.2 The Merits and Limits of the Trans-Disciplinary Approach

Concluding this critical survey of planning's different fields of activity and their emerging inter-relations it may be said that operational planning, in both the micro and macro versions, has represented the decisive factor in bringing together and integrating these fields. This has happened largely thanks to the advanced technical baggage that operational research has introduced to the various fields, which has been heavily based on mathematics and its auxiliary statistics. Therefore, operational planning has essentially been presented as a bundle of advanced techniques. It has been considered mainly of instrumental character, and thus seen as trans-disciplinary, to be applied to every field at every level from micro- to macro-programming.

3.2.1 Merits

These techniques, however, have had great merits.

Above all, they have had the merit of creating a new arena for trans-disciplinary encounters between the different fields of planning, each of which is bound to its "base" discipline: economics, political science, sociology, the environmental sciences. This has prompted a series of typically multi-disciplinary researches and analyses, largely due to the use of trans-disciplinary techniques. These research strands are beginning to look increasingly like disciplinary integration, though they still have far to go. Elsewhere I have attempted to map these using a kind of "disciplinary map"[17].

An important and symbolic high-point was the foundation of *the Socio-Economic Planning Sciences, International Journal* in 1968. During its more than 30 years of existence this journal has sought to represent a melting-pot of experiences, tearing various planning scientists from their original environments (and journals)[18].

Furthermore, these techniques have had the merit of unifying the operational approach inherent to each field of planning. In other words, it has provided a programmatic, policy- or decision-oriented, direction to the traditional base-disciplinary analysis.

The operational approach has pushed several of the strands of research that it influenced to the extent that they were liberated from their base disciplines out of the

---

[17] The "Map of Strands toward Planology" was constructed in *The Introduction to Planology* (Archibugi 1992), which has not yet been published but which is available in a provisional edition produced by the Planning Studies Centre (from which the present considerations draw a great deal).

[18] Of course, I have quoted this journal (of which I had the honour of being called to serve on the first editorial board by the founder S.N. Levine) as symbolising the vast range of new directions of research within planning, not as an exhaustive list of these. Even just considering scientific journals it would be impossible not to mention the subsequent birth of *Environment and Planning* (1969) (of which I similarly took part in the editorial board), of *Policy Sciences* (1969), and of the *Journal of Policy Modelling* (1979), not to mention the stimulating openings toward the new approaches by journals of the traditional disciplines in the fields of economics, sociology, administrative science, urban studies, and regional and environmental sciences.

latter's positivist wrappers, thereby opening up for a programmatic approach, which we will call "planological".

Nevertheless, this approach that we have defined as trans-disciplinary has shown, and will continue to present, certain limits.

3.2.2 Limits

Above all, the application of analysis and evaluation techniques to the various disciplines has prompted the development of a high level of sophistication in these techniques at the cost of adequate methodological reflection as to the validity and comprehensiveness of the results.

There has been a tendency to make *techniques* privileged, while disregarding *methods* (if I may be allowed such use of two words which are often confused)[19].

This has reduced the capacity to confront various problems critically within an adequate framework, and to avoid permanent and chronic sub-optimization[20]. Furthermore it has impeded the birth of a proper management system, even in the case of merely technical consultancy to planning processes carried out individually by analysts or planners.

In the second place, the trans-disciplinary use of these techniques may have *slowed down* fundamental change of the approaches which a thorough methodological discussion would necessarily have introduced.

This new approach would allow the emancipation of planning from the conditions of its base disciplines, which are to a great extent responsible for the malfunctioning and crisis.

Inasmuch as the new approach is the pivot of the much sought-after new disciplinary integration it merits brief discussion.

3.3 "Positivist"-Type Decision-Making Analysis

Operational analysis, as applied to economics, social plans, physical plans etc. does not impede the normative "moment"; on the contrary, it calls for it. Even the modelling on which such procedures as linear programming is based is clearly naturally oriented toward decision-making.

---

[19] By "techniques", I mean the instrumental use of mathematical language, for example formalisation through algebraic expressions (with or without the possibility of quantification), and thus modelisation of the relationships between the phenomena which have been selected for the construction of the reference system, subject to analysis and planning. By "method", I mean the identification of phenomena to select in order to shape the set of objectives or problems to be resolved (in whatever environment or state of reference); the conceptualisation of the existing relationships between these phenomena, their contents and their contexts; and the procedures for evaluation of the alternative courses of action possible in pursuit of the objectives or solutions of the identified problems.

[20] On the risk of sub-optimisation see an essay by Papandreou and Zohar (1971).

Nevertheless, the structure of the phenomena (variables) of which the model is composed, and the relationships between these phenomena (variables), are the result of the objective analysis of the system in question, be it economic, social, or physical-ecological etc., and whether it is international, national, regional or urban. The starting point is always the "positive" identification and "configuration" of reality, including the constraints it represents. This is the base on which variables are selected: target variables related to objective-values, and instrumental variables which are supposedly under the control of the decision-makers. Given the system of "positive" relationships and constraints, the decision-maker should be able to make an informed choice between alternative courses of action.

"Knowledge before decision" is the motto of this conventional approach to the problem of planning: as obvious and trivial as it is accepted and recommended. Who can deny the importance, and even necessity, of analysing and knowing the ways things work in order to be able to govern them, as if they were natural phenomena?

Economics, political science, social sciences, ecological, urban and regional studies all supply the *data* concerning which the analytical models allow prescriptions when necessary (crises, problems, concerns, etc.).

Despite its use for decision-making this approach remains "positive"[21].

3.4 Social Reality is Subjective Reality

But what is this "reality" which is so objective that it is necessary to know its functioning before going ahead with prescriptions, recommendations, choices, and decisions?

In the case of social science and planning this is not a matter of a reality of nature which has its own inviolable laws.

This is a case of a reality of *human behaviour*, the behaviour of individuals, groups, classes, ethnic and cultural groups (in the anthropological sense). This behaviour varies over time and with circumstances, and even according to moods and fashions. These are not realities for which it is possible to study and determine unequivocal laws of behaviour, either for groups or for historical moments and circumstances. Social behaviour, and thus also social objectives, are so variable as not to allow us to create models and parameters in a "positive" way.

We are dealing with a reality composed of behaviours (of individuals, groups or societies) that the decisions themselves tend to define, explain, and influence. In other words, this reality is a function of the decisions, within certain given constraints.

The "system of reality" as a whole does not, however, amount to an *independent* variable in the decision-making system. On the contrary, it is heavily dependent, not only due to the effect a decision can have on it, but also because its creation is based on the objectives recognised in the decisions.

This is not to say that there are no limits, but rather that the limits are of a structural kind rather than behavioural. There are given material resources, but the freedom of choice is complete.

---

[21] Even if not in his best clearness, I think that this conclusion has also been reached also some time ago by Marc Los (1971).

Granted, within a framework limited by time, place, and level of development, such behaviours may begin to seem similar and to feature a lot of regularity; it is certainly always worthwhile knowing past behaviour in order to judge the possibilities of the future. A number of "theories" have been formulated concerning such supposed regularities, but exaggerated scientific value has been attached to these. Indeed many calculations based on probability have proved correct; but in the case of complex decisions and choices, how can the reasoning and decision-making model be said to have a "scientific" base when the latter's assumptions are so fragile, with the uncertainty coefficient deriving from the ingenuous "scientific" method itself?

When decisions have to be made concerning the future, would a community not do better by (as individuals do) incorporating the behaviour of groups and individuals into the decision process *ex ante*, while considering methods for simulation of this behaviour, rather than reproducing set parameters obtained from uncertain data collected *ex post*?

Thus, in this case the existence of a normative approach, different from that extracted from "positive" analysis, is beginning to stand out.

3.5 "Voluntarist"-Type Decision-Making Analysis

An approach is beginning to take shape, in which the modelling of reality would be based above all on *structural* relations selected with the problems and objectives of planning. Its aims will be pragmatic rather than heuristic: to measure the technical coherence and feasibility of the choices and of the preferred set of options.

As far as behavioural decisions are concerned, these should be: a) drawn up at a desk by whomever has been charged with deciding on behalf of society; b) evaluated by similarly charged politicians; and c) subject to negotiation with interested groups and individuals who enjoy liberty and autonomy to form and express preferences, and thus affect the implementation of community plans.

Hence, the distinction between the "voluntarist" and the "positivist" approach.

From this point of view, there would be no economic behaviour that, once studied and codified in economic theory, required verification in the light of other values and criteria. Neither would there be social behaviour which, naturally belonging to social analysis, needed to be confronted with the theorems of *homo economicus*. Nor would the logic of group action have sense any longer, as an irrefutable factor obstructing any intention for the reform of social behaviour.

From this point of view, the "whole" man would choose; and in our case the whole of society would do so, or rather its legitimate representatives. The community decides, in accordance with its preference scales, that have yet to be defined, or have been determined through bargaining in accordance with established procedures. The preferences are then part of various complex values, which it is rather difficult to attribute to specific sub-systems.

In fact, the distinction between the economic, social, or political nature of things fades with the formulation of preferences, based on a well-arranged system of objectives. This is expressed in the programme structure, or a complex logical frame (log-frame) of the system of objectives.

What remains is, on one side, the (rationally expressed) objectives, and, on the other, the instruments with which to pursue those objectives. Similarly, the issue of coherence and consistency of said objectives remains, as does the question of coherence and consistency in the use of the instruments.

And, furthermore, there remains the classical relationship between objectives (the use of available resources) and the means (in terms of the availability of resources)[22].

This "voluntarist"-type approach characterises the new discipline, as it synthesises and overcomes the planning sciences and transforms them into one "planning science" (or rather, planology).

In this way, the conventional motto "knowledge before decision" is reversed, becoming "knowledge through decision". The same selection of variables for the model-building is carried out, not in deference to an "objective" reality, but rather in deference to the entirely "subjective" one, which the planners are hoping to change, inasmuch as they have constructed purpose-built problems, values, aspirations and objectives. The analysis follows a first formulation of problems and objectives, and is born as evaluations of the obstacles, difficulties, feasibility, constraints, inherent in the pursuit of these objectives. In other words, the analysis is geared toward the programme, and the only variables (and relationships between these) analysed are the ones relevant to the programme.

To summarize, the assumption, which I have developed more extensively elsewhere (see Archibugi 1992 and 1994), is that the trans-disciplinary approach, though decision-oriented, remains "positivist" inasmuch as it is anchored in the positive paradigms of the base sciences (economics, sociology, etc.). The qualitative step taken by disciplinary integration occurs as (adopting a "voluntarist" approach) planning science parts from its paradigm, i.e., that of the planning process.

During the planning process there is no distinction between the social and economic objectives which must be made compatible. The coordination happens within the decision-making process itself, which takes off from the substantial goals, of which all conditions and marginal constraints, as well as the conditions of feasibility, are operationally analysed.

The *trans-disciplinary* approach effectively becomes *neo-disciplinary*, and the new discipline frees itself completely from the old one.

3.6 A Defect of Approach or One of Further Elaboration?

The new integrated planning discipline (or planning science, or planology) must find new common bases; i.e., that are common to any plan typology (or any field of planning) to which it is applied.

Such bases consist of the consolidation of procedures of analysis, of evaluation and of decision. These are the *common store of any planner* in whichever field he or

---

[22] The most complete and probably clearest formulation of an integrated logical planning process is that of Johansen, by means of his "theoretical decision-making planning scheme" (1977, chaps. 2.1 and 2.2). There is a vast epistemological treatment of the planning cognitive process in Faludi (1986).

she works and whatever the plan being applied. Notwithstanding certain schematisms introduced by operational planning, which is above all aimed at the management of micro-units and micro-projects, these schematisms have not yet been elaborated, discussed, or consolidated enough on a complex community scale. The "facet by facet" fascination still prevails in the planner's activities; this because it is so much simpler and more easily understandable. It obtains greater consensus thanks to its banality and to the fact that it involves a less complex and intellectually more manageable vision.

Therefore, planning science has yet to be born; let alone "rethought"! Until now, we have worked in the utmost disorder. Whilst claiming to be rational, we have acted within the greatest irrationality, not only on the part of the political decision-makers (who sometimes sacrifice wisdom and duty for political success), but also on the part of the planners who should act as the critical conscience of the decision-makers. Whether on a territorial or sectorial scale, nowhere in the world do we have at our disposal reliable frames of reference that indicate the capacity to apply a methodology or even a basic "systemic" consciousness.

In Italy, if we add up the demographic predictions of the regional and local master plans produced by the illustrious profession of urban planners we will find that we should be at least a country of 300 million inhabitants. How can we have the courage to say that our planning was imbued with too much "rationalism" and that this is why it failed! The truth is that it failed because of the incompetence of those who define themselves as planners and who don't know how to begin preparing a plan; because it has been a matter of pseudo-planning (as Dudley Seers defined it as far back as 1972 in the full flowering of policy sciences and programming); and because the planners have been the first to abdicate from the task of elaborating, with due tenacity and patience (against political adversities and fashion cycles) the procedures and methods of planning evaluation.

Quantitative planning has been paralysed by the absence of data, despite the fact that the global "change" that we have lived through has aimed at making the collecting and processing of data easier. Qualitative planning has also been paralyzed by a lack of trust in gaining collective preference with suitable organisational tools and with suitable institutional procedures. Here certainly it is necessary to rethink old institutional schemes and new proposals of "constitutional engineering" that fit better with planning procedures! Even in the institutional field, the lack of confidence in rationality has led to a total lack of imagination and initiative.

Myrdal (if I remember correctly) told a conference of the American Institute of Planners held in Washington, DC, in 1968 that the most frustrated profession was certainly that of the planner, but that they should be nevertheless proud, because in the long run, by dint of their predictive, rational capacities, they would be the profession most up with the times and the one the world would have the most need of. I don't know whether Myrdal would be happy today to see the defeatism that pervades the camp, but it is certain that his claim has not lost any validity[23], even bearing in mind

---

[23] Incidentally the same is valid for Myrdal himself. In fact, during the time when the welfare state was the fashion, he went against the grain by recommending going "beyond the welfare state" with arguments that are more relevant today than they were thirty years ago. He asked

the changes that have taken place in the meantime, because today it is hard to imagine a development that is aware of international and inter-regional relations, and an efficient management of communities, without the contribution of more advanced methods of management than a day-by-day policy allows.

The role of the planner is not to be successful *hinc et nunc*, but rather that of teaching how to manage the common good, and in the first place, that of creating good planners who are capable of transmitting their professional ability[24].

I do not see such ability in planners today. Neither do I see it in our universities or in its graduates to carry out their role in the various administrative bodies. In this situation, is there even anything to fail? What failure, then, can we talk about?

I, on the other hand, see a very important task: to further refine and elaborate our discipline and to give it a more precise identity and a more organic, systematic, and greater capacity, and to integrate its various aspects. Until we are able to do this, we do not have the right to talk of failure.

---

that the welfare state be administrated with more "planning", so that the social groups became accustomed, in negotiating the plan, to making choices, implementing trade-offs, and expressing "preferences"; and not just to pressing for social services, as a political demand, that could not be sustained with an objectively limited public budget (Myrdal 1960).

[24] In this sense, Aaron Wildavski wrote wellknown, elegant and perceptive words (1973, pages 141, 145, 149 and others).

4

The First Routes of the New Discipline

As discussed in the previous chapter, the lines of further refinement and elaboration, within the logic of an integral re-establishment and unified approach, are the following:

- to elaborate and strengthen the unitary procedure scheme in the preparation of plans, with the relative indication of the phenomena (variables) to be quantified in the various phases of preparation of a typical integrated plan;
- to strengthen and define schemes of the systemic inter-relationship between the various levels of planning and thus of the various plans;
- to design institutional procedures (and relative institutions) for plan bargaining at all levels; as well as to design consultation systems of the opinions and preferences of the participants interested in the plan;
- to design (and manage) suitable information systems that correspond to the pre-selected variables and to the accounting systems instituted, (according to the previous points);
- to design monitoring and evaluation systems of the operational capacity of the plans, and of a periodical review and updating of the same.

It seems to me that the literature on planning has not produced enough in this direction: neither in the shape of proposals nor as a result of experience. In my opinion, "suitable" text books do not exist that are precise, exhaustive, and sufficiently didactic; that is, "treatises" that treat the subject systematically (as have existed in the fields of economics, sociology, and even in regional sciences, as Isard's well-known book of 1960 testifies). There are, on the other hand, many interesting papers on this or that subject, or this or that experience; there are many brilliant pamphlets, even of voluminous bulk, which are useful for the development of the critical spirit (which is certainly very important) but not for the possession of a reliable methodology. We all know that when we have had to confront the preparation of a plan we have had to invent, case by case, a new methodology *ex novo*, and that we have found little support in our libraries. Neither have we found in the documents on produced plans (apart from suggestions and hints) adequate "ideal-type" models to follow.

4.1 Schemes of Procedure for the Preparation of Plans and the Construction of Suitable "Accounting Frames"

The first field of elaboration is that of the methodology of plan preparation. In the scientific community of planners, we should discuss and formulate a standard, an ideal model to follow. Above all, this should be done with regard to which categories of "objectives" to insert in a "programme structure," which articulation of the target-instruments' linked relationship to suggest and prefer, which level of aggregation to accept for the phenomena (variables) to be quantified, and which indicators of state, of achievement, of action, etc. to identify in the diverse typologies of the community plan.

It is in this instance that one should identify and construct the models and the accounting frames to be used for all the analyses of consistency between plan alternative evaluations and plan hypotheses. The scientific community of planners have done surprisingly little in this field. There are very abstract and theoretical analyses on the subject of the building of decision-making models, of spatial interaction, of the input-output relationship, etc. but there has been little elaboration with regard to their insertion into the "entire" plan procedure. The level at which there is a greater abundance of operational models is perhaps that of the entire national economy (thanks especially to the noteworthy contribution of the methodology of input-output analysis, though it was frustrated greatly by a shameful lack of accounting data). However, at this level as well, the prevalent approach is "macro-economic", and therefore somewhat partial: the attempts to build a "system of models" for planning on a national scale with a strong correlation of variables have been nullified by scarce political and financial encouragement. The scientific community itself has not been sufficiently tenacious, so let's just imagine how the political and administrative bodies have been.

On the subject of "planning model systems", there was a UN seminar held in Moscow in 1974, which brought together the econometric experts who had been working in both Western and Eastern planning offices. The problem was discussed with all seriousness, although little in fact resulted from the seminar (see UN-ECE 1975). I have the impression, as I have said elsewhere, that this seminar was the "swan-song" for the development of planning "model systems". I presented a paper at that seminar on the Italian experience of an "integrated" formulation of a "models system" in which there was linked to a Leontiefian "central" input-output model a range of "sectorial" resource-use models (activated by a system of social indicators) that were translated into goods and services through suitable transition matrices (Archibugi 1974). The models system was a rough methodological outline of an experience that should have been developed by the (official) Istituto Italiano per gli Studi di Programmazione Economica, but was in fact cut short by the crisis in all fields of economic planning in Italy as a consequence of the oil crisis. In my opinion, for planning modelisation on a national scale the discussion should be taken up again from the point at which it was left, i.e., from the "system of models".

On the other levels, sub-national, (i.e., regional, urban, etc.) and supra-national or even on the world level, we have much less interesting examples of modelisation that are greatly misleading because of the lack of systemic binding.

There is an abundance of regional and urban models. The majority of these are "descriptive"; only a few are linked to real planning processes. Most have a "positivistic" basis: i.e., that they put knowledge before decision. Also greatly lacking is their systemic relationship with the meta-regional decisions that are so important for the regional and sub-regional life[1].

"Global" modelisations are still at an elementary and descriptive state; even that which was carried out in the general study by Leontief himself (1977) for the UN. Other studies (like those of the Club of Rome) are of a purely exploratory and "predictive" nature, and are certainly not decision-making, in the sense here underlined. Besides, they have also come to a halt because of the poor quality of the data available.

That said, in order to perceive how planning procedures could progress in the direction of this first field of elaboration one could not do better than to turn to W. Leontief's masterly essay, in which, in a plain and simple form, he explains what he understands by (national) economic planning (Leontief 1976). By following his scheme, it is very possible to construct a standard planning process also for the other relevant levels. Leontief himself set forth, in a seminar given at the Planning Studies Centre in 1964, the possible developments of planning technology (reprinted in Leontief 1966). His views have remained quite relevant, since from that time an appropriate planning methodology has not made progress.

4.2 Schemes of the Systemic Interrelationship Between Plan Levels

This is a field of elaboration that is even less frequently employed by the scientific community, perhaps as a consequence of the persistent personal separation of the individual scholars of the national level from those of the regional and urban levels.

In practice, all the "constraints" that it should be obligatory to bear in mind in the planning process (see preceding paragraph) should be listed and discussed; that is, those constraints that belong to the analysis of the phenomena of the superior or inferior level to that in which one operates. In other words, the exogenous constraints with which a plan must reckon.

In practice, this theme is normally called "plan coordination". But in the scientific sphere, it is a question of technically defining which are the exogenous co-variables of different planning models at the operational level. Without a clear and compulsory consideration of these variables, any form or experience of planning becomes "pseudo-planning". I fear that if we were to carry out a survey on the awareness of the existence of the exogenous constraints in planning experience (especially at the urban scale) over the last decades in all parts of the world, we would discover that in

---

[1] A good, classic synthesis of this type of modelling is in Wilson (1974); amongst the best "operational" structuring of modelling are those Fox has studied in more than one work: (Chap. 12, Fox et al. 1966) on the "Theory of quantitative economic policy with applications to economic growth, stabilization and planning", and in Chaps. 8 and 12 of Fox "*Social indicators and social theory: Elements of an operational system*" 1974. Fox has elaborated a very interesting system of social accounting that could be a good bridge for the integration between socio-environmental and economic accounting. See Fox 1985. The Frisch's remains however basic: see also Frisch 1964; 1971.

more than 90% of the existing plans it is completely lacking (and that this percentage strangely coincides with that of the failure rate of the said plans). This observation was made as far back as 1965 by Waterson in a work that then represented a report on the vast experience of planning (in the ambit of the World Bank). I believe that since then it cannot be said that the situation has improved, but rather that it has gotten worse.

The research and studies of the planners should arrive at (by theory or experiment) a particular "normalization" for the processes of plan preparation, in which is demanded (as terms of reference for the carrying out of a good job) the explication of the constraints and external conditions on which the analyses and "internal" evaluation of the plan are based. Such assumptions should be present either as data, or as estimates, or as simple hypotheses; they should be present, however, and also be the object of the controls and the negotiations (with the appropriate participants) just like all the other contents of the plan.

4.3 Institutional Procedures of "Plan Bargaining" and Preference Consultation Systems

Not only for their *implementation*, but also for their *preparation*, plans need to assume and presume "behaviour" and "preference" guidelines on the part of the *subjects interested* in the plan: whether they be passive subjects such as consumers, users, and in general the "target-subjects" of the plan, or the active subjects such as entrepreneurs, small or large private or public operators, trade unions, or the actual political decision-makers.

Marketing analyses are excellent tools for the evaluation *ex post* (statistical) and *ex ante* (polling) of behaviour. They have been little practiced by planners as by public operators in general; although they are much more used in "*corporate planning*". But the opinions and preferences of various interested groups can be collected and measured permanently with modern systems of control that no-one applies (it is strange that we can have TV audiences constantly monitored and yet not equip planners with a similar monitoring system for patterns of behaviour and preferences which are much more important for the political operators, and which represent decisive factors (when in the hands of planners) for the well-being of the community). But, on what can we base this monitoring if we have not beforehand constructed and organised the indicators the plans need (about which see Sect. 1)?

This does not mean that we must not also perfect the design of organised forms of plan negotiations, with certain groups and subjects being identified as strategic in the creation of a collective preference function, let alone for the subsequent implementation of the plan, and more in general for its management.

Above all, on a national scale, but also on other scales (sub- or supra-national) that repeat the constitutional scheme of the national one, the task of the scientific community is that of studying and proposing institutional and operational reforms that fit the needs of plan management. Any of today's institutional systems founded on 19th century constitutional schemes are completely incapable of carrying out the management tasks of a planning state or of a planning society; and even less of a state that has to rationalise and control its expenditure that reaches the equivalent of more than 50% of the national income (up from the approx. 5% from the middle of the last century).

The actual procedure and structure of public budgeting (of states, regions, municipalities) is based on schemes introduced in the last century, without much updating, in the main Western countries. If we don't want planning to fail, it will be necessary to elaborate a transformation and adaptation of expenditure procedures to the schemes of planning decisions.

The American experience of the PPBS at the end of the 60's has backfired, and it was the most advanced experience of adaptation of public expenditure procedures to the needs of planning in the Western world. But, although it backfired, it has left some very important traces, which are wrongly considered to be only a "deregulation" process: e.g., the principle that every administration must show that the costs of a public activity must be lower than the benefits such activity produces. The scientific community of planners must definitely relaunch, at least at a study level, processes and methods of public expenditure evaluation, as one of the most important pieces of the general planning methodology puzzle (more references to the American experience of strategic planning in the federal administration after 1993, in Chap. 7).

4.4 Information Systems for Planning and Their Management

A field that needs elaboration (and which has hardly yet begun) is the design of information systems that harmonizes with the introduced system of planning.

The application of information systems has allowed us to make great technical progress in the last few decades; we must ask why these systems haven't been introduced into planning. One reply is that progress has been made where a "demand" for information systems has arisen for existing or developing activities. Poor planning has simply not represented one of these "demand" areas. Nevertheless, one must not forget that one of the reasons for the difficulty that planning has had in presenting itself as a current practice in the administration of the community at all levels (including the national one) is the difficulty implied in managing information, both for the simple existence of sufficient data and for the capacity of processing such data (given their complexity in the general planning framework). Therefore, a potential obstacle can now be considered overcome.

In reality, information technology has not yet given all its potential and powerful support to the collecting and processing of data useful for planning, in spite of many favourable circumstances. Information about the great accounting phenomena is still insufficient and incomplete. The scientific community must make every effort to plan "accounting" systems, for the construction of which it must also identify the necessary basic data (see next Chap. 4) for integrated planning processes.

4.5 Monitoring and Plan Evaluation Systems

This, too, is a line of elaboration for the new discipline, in which there is still much to do.

In the last couple of decades there has taken place a well-known blossoming of studies and applications in all directions. Paradoxically, these studies (which complement planning to such an extent as to merit the saying: "No planning without evaluation, but no evaluation without planning") have developed concomitantly with the decline in planning studies. From an historic viewpoint (according to the fashion of the times), they have appeared as a more concrete and more realistic alternative to the (unsuccessful) planning experience. In reality, the (false) alternative for (false) planning has been the planning by "projects" that has been considered informally as a more modest and effective and less whimsical alternative to overall planning.

We know that, within an integrated and systemic approach, planning "by" projects, without systemic reference to other levels of planning, represents simply the negation of planning. The opposite also is true: comprehensive planning, not backed-up by feasibility analyses at an operational level and at the level of single projects would likewise be a negation of planning.

The flourishing of evaluation methods has been had, however, in the ambit and *humus* of project analysis of all types: from the social to that of productive investment, etc.; and it has been an instrument of that micro-projecting in which a part of operational planning has manifested itself (about which see Sect. 1.5 of Chap. 2).

A great challenge for the development of the new discipline of planning is, therefore, that of the development of the studies and methodologies of evaluation also in the ambit of macro-planning, i.e., community planning on an urban, regional or national scale. In this direction, there is a great deal of work to do. The evaluation of plans, which are still not interrelated systemically in the sense noted in Sect. 2, has ample application with the techniques suggested by an important group of scholars that is an important part of the planology strands: for example Lichfield (1975), with his method of cost-benefit analysis inserted into the formation of the "balance sheets" of evaluation; or Hill (1973), with his method of evaluation considered with respect to goal achievement, and the instruments and techniques of multi-criteria analysis and evaluation have been studied on a vast scale and there are many available.[2]

In short, the application of these methods and techniques in a wider typology of plans implies a considerable amount of study and research that is finding it hard to develop (even if, at the level of the UN and of many other agencies working in the field of project-making, traditional project evaluation has been supplanted by the evaluation of "programmes", thus presenting itself as an instrument of macro-programming).

---

[2] For example, Voogd's manual (1983) on multi-criterial analysis applied to regional and urban planning and the collection of various techniques by Sinden and Worrel (1979) for non-monetary cases.

5

Some Integrative Topics of the New Planning Discipline

In Chaps. 2 and 3, while describing some research fields aimed at an *integrated* approach to planning, and from there towards the foundation of a unitary and integrated *corpus* of methods, knowledge, and *know-how*, it has been pointed out that some *research fields* are still, necessarily, separated from the nature of traditional disciplines, and from the object itself of their researches and applications. There were envisaged some research *integrative topics*, from which, given their multi-disciplinary character, (even if still not having found a precise definition and location in a new, integrated methodology), it is believed that theory *of* planning will receive its most interesting drive.

In this chapter a first summary of these topics will be made and a first schematic description given. This is done with the conviction that research guidelines towards *planological integration* must necessarily be compared with these *topics*, in some way or another; and that only by pursuing these guidelines of research will it be possible to assure the positive development of planning theory.

Therefore, if the guidelines described in Chap. 3 of this work are for a deeper methodological integration of planning science and activity, now it will also deal with some topics that seem more urgent to face as a specific field of the new discipline, as topics that constitute some *typical contents* for an integration of approaches.

The selected topics are:

1. The integration between systems of economic accounting and systems of social accounting[1].

---

[1] We are aware that in the origins of economic accounting related to nationwide systems, this accounting has also been called *social accounting*. (See especially the preferred language of Richard Stone (1959 and 1967) and the *Department of Applied Economics* at the University of Cambridge several years ago). But, since the conventional denomination of that accounting has become *economic* or *national*, we prefer to reserve the expression *social accounting* for the new attempts to create an integrated accounting system outside the national accounting system, capable of reaching the *non-economic* (or as I would prefer, the *non-monetary*) phenomena of welfare. By this, I mean that they are not measurable with the help of actual or simulated prices of the *market*, but rather through *other* indicators of output or of utility. (See for these aspects my book: *The Associative Economy*, Macmillan 2000).

2. The integration between planning systems (and related accounting) and techno-logical forecasting.
3. The integration between socio-economic planning and physical (or environmental or spatial or land use) planning.
4. The integration between socio-economic-physical planning and institutional public planning.
5. The integration between institutional public planning and collective bargaining with private and independent planning and projecting.

As I have said above, I will identify these subjects only briefly (reserving more in-depth illustrations for another work[2]), but in a way that will be sufficient for the reader to understand what I mean by a new "general frame" for the successful development of planning activities[3], which will serve as an introduction to the next chapter.

The articulation of these study areas will be described in the following sections.

5.1 Integration Between (Conventional) Economic Accounting Systems and Social Accounting Systems

This study area is of particular importance to the new discipline. Since the "movement for social indicators" (which has carried on rather tiredly since the end of the 1960s) has lost some of its initiative, it now seems opportune to elaborate the ways of integrating social and economic accounting in order to use them in an orderly and methodical fashion, as an instrument and reference-frame for a planning process.

In reality, social indicators originally came about as instruments for reporting on the state of social affairs. The first studies were developed in this sense, and showed a number of important results within the OECD "Common Social Concerns" system (OECD 1973, 1976, 1982) as well as in the System of Social and Demographic Statistics developed by Richard Stone for the United Nations Statistics Office (UNSO 1975). Unfortunately, the former were never followed up properly within the OECD, suffering the general decline of planning studies, and for the latter an effective collection of data was, as might have been expected, never carried out.

The integration with economic accounts, which was more clearly geared toward political goals, gave birth to a series of scientific issues. Among the more illustrious

---

[2] I refer again to the *Introduction to Planology* (*first draft*, Rome 1992), in which critical illustrations have been identified of different cultural and scientific strands that have lead to the conception of an integrated and unified approach to planning. I also examine the articulation of the contents of Planology, in general, and its evolutionary relationship with other disciplines and with the fields and strands on which it is based.

[3] For many years, in co-operation with a group of colleagues and friends, I have been working to build a treatise on *general planning* (hoping to have enough time ahead in which to complete it) epitomising systematically, principles, criteria, and methods of planning at different scales and facets of community life. I believe that the best way to move towards the improved performance of planning as a new discipline (planning science or planology) is to give a systematic outline of its foundations.

examples are: the Mew (*Measurement of Economic Welfare*) by Nordhaus and Tobin (1973), and the Japanese NNW (*Net National Welfare*) by the Economic Council (1973). The various "integrated" systems of social accounting have since been discussed (see Juster and Land 1981); of these I draw attention to Fox and Gosh (1981) and Terleckyi (1981) in particular. The work of Karl Fox is of fundamental importance to this direction. He presented a System for Social Accounting (1985) which could have been widely applied (statistically), had planning been more advanced. Furthermore, Fox's work is evidence of how multi-disciplinary accounting may yield fruits wholly independent of the "base" (original) disciplines (see Fox and Miles 1983).

Finally, the socio-economic integrated model developed by Drewnowski (1970) in the UNRISD (*UN Research Institute for Social Development*) framework should be mentioned as a step toward the modelling of integrated plans. In Drewnowsky, one sees the most extensive work on quality of life planning (1974).

Despite the undeniable progress already made by Drewnowsky's work, a lot remains to be done in order to standardise procedures, thus providing planners with adequate and useful standard schemes. This is a study area which it should be very fruitful for the new discipline to cover. A summary of the themes of this area could be as follows:

1. an increasingly developed *theorization of social indicators*; considering the ways in which the needs, welfare, demands and aspirations (of individuals, groups, the community, public authorities) relevant to the objectives can be measured. This can be done in connection with the contents of the programme structure (see next section);
2. the *forms and techniques for extending the conventional economic system of accounts* (SNA – System of National Accounting), which the UN has been discussing, reforming and updating (in 1995). The aim is not merely to get a more complete measurement of welfare and development, but also measurements which are more operational with respect to planning systems' goals;
3. the *modelling* to be used to link social objectives and their measurements to traditional (conventional, for instance input-output; or "new") accounting systems.

5.2 Integration Between Socio-Economic Planning (and Related Accounting) and Technological Forecasting

This still developing area of the new discipline is composed of studies of the following:

1. updating (and methods connected to this) the *technical coefficient matrix* in conventional input-output accounting systems, using the findings of technological forecasting;
2. *integration of technological matrices and professional labour factor matrices*;
3. methods of iteration and of *evaluation of interactive relationships between technological forecasting and socio-economic planning* (this area could be called "technological planning").

As is the case with many other study areas of the new discipline, this whole area is heavily conditioned by the availability of information which, at the moment, is far from satisfactory. Thus, the first task of this area must be to identify the nature and potential sources of the necessary information, in order to render the contents of this area operative.

5.3 Integration Between Socio-Economic Planning (and Related Accounting) and Physical (or Territorial or Environmental) Planning

This area covers the many aspects of the relationships between spatial and physical factors and the non-spatial and non-physical factors of development.

The themes developed in this area have their base in the works of the so-called *regional sciences*. However, they need to be rearranged subject to the heuristic logic of planning theory (as outlined above in Sect. 1). The following are the most relevant of these themes:

1. the *modelling of the component of spatial accessibility to economic well-being*;
2. the *translation of environmental values into the terms of socio-economic values (and of economic accounting)*;
3. the *measurement and evaluation of environmental and urban quality* (environmental indicators and the *urban effect*);
4. *construction methods of matrices of the demand and supply of territory*;
5. integration of *territorial accounting (usage values and dis-values) and accounting of transport (cost-benefit for firms and for users)*.

It cannot be denied that the "environmentalist" fashion today (and the "regionalist" one of yesterday) have prompted great investigation and reflection in this study area, as well as extensive literature, even though the latter is conceptually very disorganised. Within the new discipline, the matter is also (beyond the continuation of this fervour of studies toward increasingly better approaches) better-aimed research. This, in order to square the research increasingly methodologically with the preparation of physical-territorial plans, which are again compatible with the socio-economic reference frames (of Sect. 1). This connection between the socio-economic and physical-territorial frames constitutes one of the pillars of the new discipline.

5.4 Integration Between Socio-Economic (and Physical) Planning and Institutional Organisation and Negotiation

This area of the new discipline covers the many aspects of the relationship between conditions, constraints, institutional objectives, and the technico-economical feasibility of plans on one side, and the more general social limits to the rationality of the planning process on the other. The following lines of research may be listed:

1. the in-depth *examination and accounting disaggregation of the flow and economic-financial transactions between institutional "sectors" (agents) in economic accounting*;
2. the *analysis of the conditions connected to the behaviour of the sectors and of the institutional agents concerning flows* (savings, investment, access to the capital market, fiscal levy, psychological effects of transfers, etc.) *in connection with the processes and objectives of planning*;
3. *new forms of work and consumption* (forms of auto-production and auto-consumption, non-profit economy, etc.) that are non-commercial and not-for-profit and their role in the formation and distribution of "informal" income.

The "third sector", or "associative economy" (there are many names to define very similar activities: for example, informal economy, non-profit economy, "economie sociale", and so on) has developed as an effect and, indeed, as a counter-effect of the welfare state, at least in its most present instantiation, and since the welfare state is in crisis because it lacks planned and controlled demand for public services, the increasing volume of activities of the third sector could be "programmed" within a framework of planning decisions. For a wider consideration on the relationship between the Planning perspective and the increased third sector, see my work on the associative economy (Archibugi, 1985 and 2000a). Until now, this area has been "compartmentalised", whereas it ought to be included in the institutional modelling of plans, and relative accounting, to an increasing extent[4].

5.5 Integration Between Socio-Economic Planning and the Institutional System and Design

This area of the new discipline is a part of any kind of research that aims to elaborate on the relationship between the technical content of planning processes and methods on the one hand, and procedures for political decision-making on the other. The latter is obviously connected to various existing juridical, administrative and public arrangements.

This is an ill-defined field, which has ranged from the narrowly technical-juridical to the more generic issues of politics and the sociology of political life. The lines of research of the topic area can be divided as follows:

1. examination of methods for the non-institutional participation of citizens, users, and others in the planning processes;
2. the examination of methods of political "procedure" in socio-economic and territorial planning, such as: the relationship between government and parliament; the relationships between public and "social" powers (e.g., unions, consumers, etc.);

---

[4] Unification of the institutional process has been put forward in outline by myself, though it has not garnered much attention. See a report I carried out for a meeting of the International Association of Administrative Sciences, on accounting and institutional instruments of a new form of planning (Archibugi 1978).

inter- and infra-governmental relationships, between various operational levels of planning; methodologies of plan-bargaining with large corporations and meso-economic powers;[5]

3. the use of "technologies" for political evaluation of plans and "rational" choice. This includes the various aspects of cost-benefit analysis, multi-criteria analysis etc., not from the point of view of techniques used, but rather considering the way the techniques used have developed and come to express the value-judgements and preferences of the political participants.

My conclusion is that only after realising that the theory of planning must march in these multiple directions, can we say that the theory of planning exists and is useful.

5.6 Concluding Remarks: The "Planological Approach"

The study areas which have been listed here in summarised form (which all merit *ad hoc* treatment) are integrated areas of a study based on the adoption of a *neo-disciplinary* approach, free of its disciplinary background. We have called this approach "planological", thus distinguishing it from the disciplines from which it has freed itself.

The general, as well as specifically epistemological, characteristic of this approach has been discussed in Chaps. 3 and 4.

Chapter 4, in particular, attempted to trace the main routes along which the new discipline, "planning science" (in the singular form), or Planology, has developed. The areas covered by this new discipline, as listed in summary form in the previous section, are all of "integrated" character, taken from different fields of various disciplines. They all have one common characteristic which allows them to belong to the new discipline: they are "plano-centric". In other words, they are explicitly aimed at the preparation and implementation of plans. This implies an over-turning of analysis in many of these fields. Above all, this poses the problem of the decision-making, and thus of the plan, at the base of each form of analysis of the kind evoked here, including integrated forms. This is what makes up the "planological" approach, which it is so difficult to introduce into current positive analysis of reality, yet which is a distinctive part of the new approach.

It is not the task of this book to illustrate motivations and theoretical foundations of the planological approach. Neither is it the task of this book to examine in detail the disciplinary contributions that have led, are leading, and will lead, to the planological approach[6].

---

[5] For a clear delineation of a type of indicative and democratic planning that involves, with negotiation and participation, all citizens, allow me to refer to that which I made a while ago, together with Stuart Holland and Jacques Delors, on the political conditions for a development of planning itself (Archibugi et al. 1978). See also the prospects outlined on the occasion of the Ispe Forum on a new economic and social policy in Europe in 1982 (Archibugi 1982).

[6] This is the task of a forthcoming book of mine, dedicated exactly to the *programming approach*, which is very poorly practised both in economic and in urban policy and planning.

This book has the task, at least it is my intention, to only enlighten with regard to the shortcomings and the mistakes that have been manifested in that peculiar wave of researches and comments, which is named "planning theory". Planning theory has had a blooming development in the last decades, with very scarce practical or scientific results. It is, however, only one wave among many flowing towards a new disciplinary approach of planology. It must find, furthermore, its own reconstruction, if we don't wish its total decomposition.

This book intends only to trace some guidelines of such reconstruction; and in the next chapter, I will sketch the essential bone structure of a functionality which could be rational, coordinated, and methodologically consistent.

With this intention, we would not go too much on the methodological approach. Perhaps it is not a bad idea to sum up this approach with the words and authority of the founder of econometrics, Ragnar Frisch, who in the period of its scientific matu- rity, refusing the development of those studies, has supplied the first epistemological basis of the programming approach and of the planning method. On the occasion of a critical review of economic forecasting and planning, to which people thought, and also today commonly (and wrongly) think that the econometric studies should be aimed, he said:

> During the last generation the shift from the onlooker viewpoint to the decision view-point has become more and more relevant in economic thinking all over the world as witnessed, for instance, by the worldwide United Nations survey "Evaluation of long-term economics projects" (E 3379, 1960). In most countries the shift of viewpoint is, however, based on a kind of half-logic which I have never been able to understand and which, I think, will never be able to yield fundamental solutions. On the one hand, one still retains the onlooker viewpoint, and tries to make projections on this basis (growth models of the current types), and on the other hand, one will afterwards try to use such projections as a basis for decisions. How can it be possible to make a projec-tion without knowing the decisions that will basically influence the course of affairs? It is as if the policy maker would say to the economic expert: "Now you, expert, try to guess what I am going to do, and make your estimate accordingly. On the basis of the factual information I thus receive I will then decide what to do". The shift from the onlooker viewpoint to the decision viewpoint must be founded on a much more coherent form of logic. It must be based on a decision model, i.e., a model where the possible decisions are built in explicitly as essential variables (Frisch 1962, pp. 91–92).

The building of such decisional models (obviously coordinated amongst themselves by a "system of models") in all areas of study, evoked in this and previous chapters, continues to be the essential and typical task of the new discipline.

In fact, the application of these methods and techniques in a more extended ty-pology of plans, induces a considerable amount of study and research, that still needs to find its full autonomous and conscious development.

In the next chapter, I will indicate the basic postulates that, according to me, should preside over their development, and I will outline a logical frame (log-frame) within which these studies could achieve their systemic connection.

6

Planning Science: Basic Postulates and Logical Framework for Reference

6.1 From Planning "Theory" to Planning "Science"

Chapter 1 examined the vast debate amongst teachers and operators over the causes of the evident failures of planning, and over the modalities to correct the approaches to planning (on the part of planners, teachers and practitioners) in order to improve the operational effectiveness of carried-out experiences. I have manifested the worry that this vast debate (which has assumed the name "planning theory") does not lead toward anything, unless a discouraged and desperate abandonment of any application of planning principles.

In Chap. 1, I explained the reason why, for a substantial period, I personally refrained from entering into that debate: I felt the risk of being caught up in a relatively useless rigmarole. In other words, of being dragged towards a dangerous meta-analysis that, if mistaken for the possible contents of planning theory, would a) make planning theory impertinent and unfit with respect to the clarity and effectiveness that has accompanied its birth as an academic discipline, and b) additionally impair the significance and effectiveness of planning activities which planning theory intended (and I think still intends) to be a methodological support.

Therefore, in Chap. 1, I focused my attention on explaining the reasons behind the mistakes that (in my opinion) had emerged in planning theory since its noble and well-intentioned birth[1]. In addition, I synthetically tried to indicate in the further chapters of this book (Chaps. 2 to 5) the substantive fields of a conceptual and cognitive integration that could and should become the specific and cultural terrain of a renovated "planning theory".

On the basis of a criticism of current trends of the debate on *planning* theory, it is time now to go ahead in designing the logical *framework* which could imple-

---

[1] Even if the theoretical reflections on planning have remote roots in time (see an excursus of mine on this topic in a paper from 1992), I believe that among the first works inaugurating a systematic exploration of planning is that of Andreas Faludi, (1973a), accompanied by the well-known anthology of some previous works which were intended to serve as a background to it (Faludi 1973b).

ment the desired advancement towards a greater integration of the different planning approaches; and to achieve a greater integration between *procedural and substantive* planning.

In this chapter, therefore, I will try to build a framework, through which it may be possible to establish stable links between the procedural and epistemological planning with the various substantive aspects of planning, and to get a *unitary methodological scheme*.

Before that, however, in order to clear the way and to delimit the field on which to build these unitary methodological schemes we will fix some essential postulates from which we need to start in planning matters so as to give a logical order to the building of this framework. Further, that scheme will be the subject of this chapter.[2]

6.2 A reference Framework for Planning Science: Some Essential Postulates

First of all, I need to *delimit* the terrain of what we have called the new discipline of "planning science", in respect of what I perceive as an excessive extension, and excessive meta-analysis (of a philosophical-politiological type) of the planning theory, however useful and fecund these extensions may be[3]. I apply these limits by means of the old scholastic method of establishing some "postulates," i.e., assertions not discussed but taken for granted as the basis of reasoning.

6.2.1 Logical Postulates

Postulate No. 1 of a planning theory may be formulated as follows:

> PLANNING THEORY IS ESSENTIALLY BASED ON ACTION-ORIENTED ANAL-
> YSIS AND DOING, RATHER THAN ON OBSERVATION-ORIENTED ANALYSIS
> AND BEING.

By "analysis" we mean any kind of reflection, any kind of reasoning, aimed at improving knowledge and making it more effective. In the case of planning theory, the knowledge we seek is that which is useful for action, for deciding what *should or has to be done*, rather than for merely describing *what is*[4]. This is the distinction commonly drawn between "normative analysis" and "positive analysis". The conventional

---

[2] Which constitutes a further, more developed, but still approximate step toward the awaited treatise on the foundations of the planning sciences.

[3] To which we made reference in the previous paper (Sects. 3.2 and 3.3).

[4] This distinction, in philosophy, is as old as philosophy itself: It is the distinction between "to be" and "should be"; between "the truth" and "the good" or "the useful"; between "science" and "ethics"; or, in economics, between "science" and "art", theory and policy, political economy and economic policy. A modern treatment of the problem has been developed by some theorists of "operational research," among the best of which is that by C. West Churchman (1971) and of P.B. Checkland (1981). At IIASA (August 1980) some operational research specialists debated, together with philosophers and social scientists, the "scientific" base itself

approach of all operative sciences (those sciences, like planning, which involve decisions and actions and are connected in some way to practical activities) is to guide normative analysis through the application of knowledge gleaned from positive analysis[5]. It is presumed in these sciences that, in order not to violate "reality," normative analysis should be based *on* the positive analysis which is seen as a required premise for policy. The simple axiom is: "To know in order to act (or to decide) well." Knowledge from positive analysis is also considered to be the indispensable basis for the feasibility of action plans or programmes.

Nonetheless, action-oriented (or decision-oriented) analysis introduces a new (say, epistemological) element into consideration: the observation-oriented (or positive) analysis is itself impacted (even conditioned) by the action-oriented (normative) analysis. This is a result of the well-known "problem-solving" approach, in which the variable choice (and the relations between variables) is conditioned by a feasibility analysis, that is itself based on hypothetical behaviours (since they refer to human and social behaviours) and that are never axiomatically "positive"[6].

Now is not the time to delve deeper into the character of the "normative" approach to planning, in respect to that usually used for the natural sciences.[7] It is sufficient to assert its pre-eminence as a postulate of planning theory for any type of analysis and for the evaluation of planning itself. Whilst in other traditional social sciences (political science, economics, etc.) it may be posited, however questionable the proposition may be, that there exists a positive analysis distinct and separate from a normative analysis, in planning (and in its "science") nothing is positive, and all is entirely "normative"[8]. Also implicit is the presumption that the behaviour of phenomena is entirely

---

of operational research, within which was reproduced the same ancient methodological and epistemological dilemma: between "positivist" and "normativist" approaches. On that occasion, a vast consensus settled on the need for operational research, which I consider from the methodological point of view to be very similar to that of strategic planning (and which I call a "programming" or "planological" approach), to be freed from any illusion of being founded on a preventive positivist approach based on the findings (empirical or theoretical, it doesn't matter) of rules, constants, or, why not, laws of behaviour. (See the collection of papers from the cited meeting at IIASA in the volume edited by Rolfe Tomlinson and Istvan Kiss (1984), especially the introductory papers by Kindler and Kiss (1984), by Checkland (1984), and by Farkas (1984); and finally the last paper of Rolfe Tomlinson (1984)).

[5] For a general vision of the distinction between "positive" and "normative" in the traditional sense, in the evolution of economic thinking, see Chap. 1 of the work by Hutchinson (1964), which has rightly become a classic on the subject.

[6] This is the conclusion reached by the "rethinking" of the epistemological basis of operational research, of which we have spoken in note 4 with related citation of sources.

[7] For a deeper analysis of the question see, among others, a very beautiful essay by Gunnar Myrdal (1972) on "*How scientific are the social sciences?*".

[8] The fact that "normative" has been used in the past as a necessary complement of "positive" might produce a misunderstanding of my statement that, in planning, all is entirely "normative". It may be more useful to change the word, and to state that all is "programmatic", i.e., nothing may be based on past experience as a source of "objective" rules or laws of behaviour. On the contrary, all should be based on decisions or actions looking toward the future, including, obviously, the constraints always operating in the future, as a combina-

dependent on decisions or actions, and that it is therefore illogical to assume the opposite. Such illogical thinking is what Ragnar Frisch amusingly called "half-logic".[9]

From the definition of Postulate No. 1 defined above, we may derive another, absolutely trivial postulate[10] (Postulate No. 1-plus) as follows:

PLANNING THEORY PRESUPPOSES AN EX-ANTE ANALYSIS, AND NOT AN EX-POST ANALYSIS.

This postulate, it seems to me, excludes from consideration many of the wanderings over past experience to which planning theory often abandons itself. These wanderings, always interesting and sometimes useful to know, nonetheless introduce the risk, not to be underestimated, of defining as data (during the decision process) facts which were surely non-existent in the ex-ante reality in which any decision process is applied. Such focus on past events, moreover, results in diminished capacity for the examination of more relevant and prevalent existing data, i.e., that data inherent to the set of decisions involved and pertaining to *new* problems that arise and need to be solved. Never has it been more dangerous, as it is in the field of planning, to look at the past!

Postulate No. 2 of planning theory, I think, may be formulated as follows:

THE ACTION-ORIENTED ANALYSIS IS ESSENTIALLY ORIENTED TOWARD OPTIMISATION.

This postulate derives directly from the first. If the analysis is *ex-ante* action-oriented, and not oriented toward the analysis of things observed more or less *ex-post*, then any constraints on the decisional objectives disappear. These objectives cannot aim at anything other than to achieve the best possible result (given the constraints) regarding the objectives[11].

The fact that in the reality (*ex-post*) this optimisation is not obtained, or is obtained in a limited way, does not have any relevance for the true planning theorist. Outcome may concern the *temporis acti* analysis, but certainly not the *temporis agendi* analysis. It may interest the onlooker or, say, the historian of human behaviour, but not someone who must prepare a plan or help suggest planning decisions.

This postulate should cut off, *as falling outside the terrain of planning theory*, all of the endless discourses on the "bounded rationality", which so widely occupy the political science scene of our time. Even if we were to admit, although I personally

---

tion of the preferences, more or less negotiated, among different alternatives of decisional packages (I owe to this specification the inducement of some objections by E.R. Alexander).

[9] See the phrase quoted from Frisch at the end of the previous chapter.

[10] This postulate is so trivial that in my classroom we call it the "stupid" postulate! But, sometimes, even teachers forget and neglect stupidity!

[11] The word "optimisation" expresses in all languages that concept of maximum result, subject to the conditions, that is the foundation of rationality, and that may be also expressed by the word "effectiveness" and/or "efficiency". It is a question, therefore, of a relationship that has had and still has many nomenclatures (all equivalent, for our purposes) among them are: aim/mean; goal/constraint; result/effort; product/factor; output/input; benefit/cost; performance/resources; and so on.

would be reluctant to concede it[12], that a "positive" approach could be developed in the human and social sciences, i.e., that an *ex-post* scientific analysis of behaviours and the determination of regular behaviours (determined, according to some people, directly from the "theory" i.e., the innate "rationality" of the behaviours) could be free from logical error, all this would have nothing to do with planning theory, as a consequence of the two postulates described above. It may be relevant for the (positivist) "sciences of being", but not for a "science of action" (or praxeology)[13] such as planning.

What meaning could a "bounded" rationality have for the planner or the planning theorist? In the moment when he or she should "decide", can we imagine our planner saying, "*The best solution is that one: but I am satisfied with, or I prefer this other one which is not the best... Why? Don't ask me, because I don't know!*" In fact, if the planner or decision-maker was able to know why, he or she would have the duty of including the reason for the choice in the list of objectives he or she were pursuing, and in the trade-offs (i.e., "optimisation") between such objectives that any decision inevitably involves.

We may admit, in practice, that the decision-maker may be unconsciously unconscious of her or his preferences; but whether he or she could be consciously unconscious is a question which concerns psychiatry (even more than psychology)!

What relevance could a "bounded" rationality have for the planner who exists just to make conscious and explicit the motivations and goals of the decision-makers or the planners themselves? Indeed, exactly how could a bounded rationality concern the planning theorist, who orders the process by means of delineating the best or the most effective decisional system for the planner, remains an academic mystery!

According to the logic of Postulate No. 2, all discussion of the concept of "rationality", Cartesian or non-Cartesian, bounded or non-bounded, falls outside the terrain of planning theory. Such discussion pertains directly to the fields of philosophy and epistemology (for which I do not believe planners are especially well equipped).

6.2.2 Field or Delimitation Postulates

The first two postulates enunciated above pertain to all sorts of planning (from the more universal to the more specific). Since planning theory usually refers to the sort of planning which *grosso modo* is ranged under the common name of public (or com-

---

[12] It does not seem legitimate to me to raise a doubt of this sort here in the venue of planning theory. Instead, this should be raised in the venue of general political science oriented towards a "positivistic" approach. In any event, see one of my papers on the "Programming Approach," concerning the contribution of Ragnar Frisch, Jan Tinbergen and Wassili Leontief on this matter (Archibugi 1999); and the already cited essay by Gunnar Myrdal (1972).

[13] I state that the roots of such an assertion can be found in most of the "American" theory of society: overall in Talcott Parsons (1937 and 1951; with E.A. Shils 1961 and 1968); but also in the American philosophy of knowledge (or pragmatism): overall in Dewey (1944) or in C.L. Lewis (1946). The foundations of Praxeology, as we know, were defined later: Kotarbinski (1965) and Kaufmann (1968).

munitarian, or collective) planning, postulate No. 3 is useful for freeing the terrain of many equivocal and diverting discourses:

THE SUBJECT OF (PUBLIC, COMMUNITARIAN, COLLECTIVE, ETC.) PLAN-
NING IS AN (OFFICIALLY LEGITIMATE) COLLECTIVE ENTITY.

Or, expressed differently:

THE DECISION MAKER OF PUBLIC PLANNING IS AN INSTITUTION.

To Postulate No. 3, specific to the field of public planning, we may append a number of corollaries (or propositions of immediate deduction) which should be recalled and kept in mind during our search for a specific field of planning theory:

1. The "planner" is, by logical extension, that institution (i.e., that public entity) which is officially recognized and legitimated[14].
2. The expert-consultant, whom we usually call the "planner," himself constitutes the proxy of the institution[15].
3. The "planning society" is a system of institutions[16].
4. Since the planning society is a system of institutions, the problem of bridging the gap between individual and abstract social preferences becomes irrelevant[17]. The sole bridging-mechanism that planning theory can and should recognize is that

---

[14] By official legitimisation, we do not refer to "stamped paper" or "red tape," but to the existence of an official title to represent the will and the interest of societal groups and categories of citizens.

[15] In this way, as the advocate of any person (individual or juridical), he or she identifies him or herself with the interests of that institution as such, by associative willingness or constitutional system.

[16] Let me recall a definition of the planning society by the National Committee on National Growth Policy Processes (USA) created jointly by the American President and Congress in 1976: "The Committee does not advocate a *planned* society. We urge that America become a *planning* society. In the long run, we believe that intelligent planning will actually reduce burdensome governmental intervention in matters affecting the private sector. Much governmental interference in the economy now consists of *ad hoc* reactions to situations which have been rendered acute because they were ignored until they became intolerable. With the benefits of foresight, the Committee expects that any necessary government intervention will be more readily considered, more timely, and less heavy-handed. This need not be a complicated process. Americans can resolve that any process we create will be compatible with freedom, and will preserve, to the greatest extent possible, the widely dispersed initiative and creativity we value so highly. The oppressively technocratic and centralised atmosphere that has surrounded the image of planning can and should be put behind us." (USA-Advisory Committee on National Growth Policy Processes, *Forging America's Future: Strategies for National Growth & Development, Report*, GPO, 1977, pp. 11–12). See also the final chapter, The Planning Society, with which Faludi closes his well-known book, *Planning Theory*, 1973.

[17] It has been assumed in the old "welfare economics" (by Pigou and followers) before the "impossibility theorem" (by Arrow and the "social choice school"). For a master treatment of the issue, see Frisch (1976) and Johansen (1977).

of the "political system." Instead of speaking about "social preferences," it is more suitable and appropriate to speak of "political preferences".

5. The planning expert-consultant is committed to "rationalising" (i.e., analyzing the consistency) and coordinating the decisions of the institutions for which he is working, by means of the formulation of "plans" which are the outcome, precisely, of interactions or co-operative processes between policy-makers and analyst-planners.

6. As the number of political institutions, at all levels, responsible for planning activity increases, so increases the number of institutions involved in the planning process. The task of the expert-planner becomes the formulation of draft-plans for the decision-makers (in the context of the above-stated interactive or co-operative processes) which take into account the appropriate levels of decision (or of decisional consistency among these levels).

7. The expert-planner, consequently, must be able to rationalise and resolve possible conflicts between different institutions and compensate for inconsistencies or incongruities between different levels of decisional competency. The greater the number of institutions or decisional levels in a given society, the greater the need for planning (which is the rationalisation and optimisation of unlike and often opposed preferences between decision-makers)[18].

In sum, the postulates (and especially their corollaries which have particular resonance for the planning theorist) should be considered as such and accepted as the basis of planning theory. To ensure that planning theorists do not get dragged into debates beyond their scientific competence, and in order to guarantee that they do not stray from the research and identifications which are their own proper field of study and consultancy, these postulates should therefore be taken for granted and exempted from further debate.

Therefore, in what direction should planning theorists focus their visual scope, using as a starting point the three postulates stated above? I will try to reconstruct here the essential lines of a new planning theory, choosing deliberately a broad approach, and also a very provisional exemplification, in order to not leave the positive aspect of such effort completely in the dark.

With the help of these basic postulates and corollaries, which allow the theorist to free himself from a number of extraneous and diverting discourses of a "polity-type", I will sketch the outlines of a true planning theory, comprising both its appropriate process and contents. In this work, I will sketch a summary and essential model of this realm, proposing to leave for future works the piece-by-piece description of its features (descriptions at which I will hopefully arrive in cooperation with my colleagues).

---

[18] This corollary goes against a popular opinion that planning is possible when institutional and political freedoms are scarce and the decisional levels are few. From the corollary, instead, we derive that it is precisely the natural clashing of interests and inconsistency coming from the institutional pluralism, (as from, in general, the decisional decentralisation which prevails in the so called "market") that requires a larger co-ordination and rationalisation of decisions, i.e., planning.

6.3 The Planning Process

The definition, study, and analysis of the planning process can, in my opinion, be considered the proper task, realm, and field of planning theory. It is, moreover, the area in which we have achieved the most progress (before many planning theorists became diverted by questions beyond the theory's proper boundaries)[19]. Faludi, whom I consider the first complete "systematiser" of planning theory, dedicated the essential and by far the largest part of his work to the planning process and its various issues. In short, planning process analysis is a recognized and well-cultivated field of planning theory.

Personally, I would have very little to add to the efforts already performed, except to recommend absorbing from the best schemes extant, the sharp distinction between the various phases of planning, i.e., between the "selection phase" and the "implementation phase," within the planning process as a whole[20]. I have followed this advice myself in my textbook on the *Principles of Regional Planning* (1980) from which I here take (with some minor adaptations) the following very simplified scheme of the planning process (Fig. 6.1). I consider it particularly useful for its clear depiction of the different levels and phases of the planning process, which is so essential to the correct development of current discourses on planning.

The scheme in Fig. 6.1 lays out the basic moments and subjects of planning according to two main functions: the *selection* or choice of a plan, and the *implementation* of a plan. Such a simplified scheme, of course, requires adaptation for its application to real circumstances. Indeed, its working system is applied at every stage or level of planning (since there is almost always a superior and inferior level at any stage which can sensibly reshape the process as a whole). It is necessary to locate the process within its practical context and implement it with respect to the relevant exogenous circumstances, such as the actual level of decision, and the way the political system can modify or alter the nature of either its decision-makers, or the participants in the planning process as negotiators (stake holders), or the final beneficiaries or "target people," or the intermediary operators, and so on.

---

[19] This is also the field where planning theory, before being configured as an autonomous field of research (say, with Faludi), had many scholars working from related disciplines (for instance, system analysis and policy sciences) who could be considered the forerunners of planning theory. It is not by chance that Faludi himself, as many others before and after him (e.g., Chadwick, McLoughlin, Catanese, Cooke, Peter Hall, etc.; see some writings of the mentioned authors in the bibl. ref.) have all used schemes (more or less didactic) already proposed by some of these forerunners. (On the various disciplinary components confluent into planning theory and into new discipline which I would call "planology," see other writings of mine (1992, 1996, 1998a, b and c).)

[20] This distinction between the selection and implementation phases was recommended insistently and continually by Frisch, one of the forerunners of planning theory, in his late writings on the methodology of economic planning, republished posthumously in 1976. For comments on this distinction, see also Johansen (1977) and Archibugi (1999).

6.4 The Planning System

One place where planning theory has achieved only minor results compared with what might have been accomplished, is in the substantive side of analysis. By "substantive", I mean especially that part of analysis which is concerned with a deeper probing of the links and the integrative aspects between the different types and scales of planning. If the different planning applications, or plans (or planning typologies) such as welfare, development, housing, health, or accessibility (as "types"), and suburban, regional, national, or international (as "scales") represent the substantive side of planning, then their functional interrelationships, their interdependence, are what we mean by the substantive side of planning theory. Unfortunately, this side of the theory, as asserted repeatedly above, has been too often neglected by planning theorists, to the detriment of the implementability and feasibility of the plans.

Such damage derives, in short, from the fact that the evaluation and implementation of the "optimalities" of any type of individual plan decisions and choices, (and the capacity to apply these decisions and choices), depends heavily upon the decisions, choices, and capacity of other substantive plans. As a result, a systematic and organic co-ordination of the planning process of an individual plan with the planning process of other plans in the operational environment constitutes an essential factor and condition in the success or failure of any kind of planning.

Despite ample evidence of this *interdependence*, relationships between the different substantive plans remain very weak. Attempts at ordering these relationships into a common "planning system" (which could have been the proper, most important field of a well-intended planning theory), remain even more scarce.

I will here try to *modelise* this "planning system" in order to indicate the type of analysis and reflection I consider to be the proper field and realm of planning theory (like that of the planning as process, examined above), and upon which, in my opinion, we should found its "reconstruction".

Even here, of course, the "modelisation" or "schematisation" is oversimplified. The single items or "entries" used to articulate the different dimensions are quite tentative and provisional. They serve as indications and impressionistic suggestions on which further work on the reconstruction of planning theory should be focused.

What I find necessary to insist, from here on, is that a clear distinction be drawn between the selection stage and the implementation stage, even in the modelling of a planning system. In fact, I consider this distinction so essential that I suggest two parallel schemes for modelling the planning systems: one for each function and stage. As will be seen, however, we should not exclude or even underestimate the importance of defining a tight and actual interdependence between the two schemes.

To be clear, the planning system, which we begin to define and describe, has nothing to do with the "positive" analysis of society, or societal analysis, of which we have many examples (for instance Parsons[21], Isard[22], and many others), even if there is some similarity between them. In short, the planning system is not concerned with

---

[21] The "social system" by Parsons (1937).
[22] The "general theory" by Isard (1969).

the existing "social structure" as such; rather, it is concerned with society's management and planning[23].

The planning system is a complex system[24]. In other words, it is a system that concerns the entire social life and includes all the possible decision-makers that act within it. It is a *holistic* system. As such, it must be designed according to a model which takes into account all the possible fields of decision-making and all decision-makers who play a role in social life. It has a territorial dimension which is "global" in the literal sense: it extends to the planetary scale.

The planning system must be "structured" through a conglomerating taxonomy, evidently multi-dimensional, that is commensurate with its complexity. Multi-dimensionality, while fitting with the complexity of the system, is unfortunately at odds with the dictates of managerial practicality, and with the need for rapid identification and comprehension of the interrelationships on the part of operators, planners, or decision-makers. This is why a taxonomy that is limited in dimensions and in the extension of items is more suitable for our needs. Nonetheless, the dimensions, extension, and nomenclature (i.e., systematic naming) of the taxonomy are all quite arbitrary, and it would be advantageous for them to become planning theory's field of intense and positive study. It would also be highly useful if, after a suitable period of critical debate, planning theorists could agree upon a common, conventional taxonomy[25] in order to render it more "user-friendly" within a systematic framework of the interdependencies, and in order to facilitate faster communication and comprehension within the planners' scientific and professional communities.

In order to facilitate the understanding of what I mean by a planning system, I will design a model of only three dimensions which I believe is sufficient to include a holistic taxonomy that adequately explains the main planning features. This system, as I stated, will be divided into two models representing the two basic functions and stages of the planning process: the selection stage and the implementation stage. In addition, the system will be split according to temporal dynamics.

Needless to say, it would be possible to merge the two systems (according to the process and the temporal dynamics) into a single multi-dimensional model expressed mathematically by a hypermatrix. Such an exercise, however, might jeopardise or diminish something of the model's explanatory potential without offering increased clarity in return[26].

---

[23] This is the reason why planning theory does not need to be flanked by a theory of society (as argued by Dyckman in the quotation included, and contested by me, in Chap. 1).

[24] Truly this seems a tautology; any system is complex by definition.

[25] How useful it would be if some professional and academic associations, after adequate debate, would go so far as to agree on such a taxonomy, and related glossary!

[26] Except for the case, unlikely at the moment, of a usage in quantitative versions (with related mathematical modelling) for which, at the present, I can't see the utility. Among the most interesting modelisations (inevitably of a "holistic" character) which I met in the planning literature is that well-known work by D.L. Foley (1964), included in the effort of M.M. Webber (1964) to explore the a-spatial aspects of the urban structure (and already used in my handbook on regional planning, 1979). I have the impression that the roots of the Webber/Foley model, strongly anchored in urban studies, have also clearly constrained it, as well as the other important quantitative spatial modelisations of the literature: for instance those

6.4.1 The Planning Selection System

As identified above, planning selection is one of the most important stages of the planning process (see Fig. 6.1). It serves as the basis of the "strategic" nature of planning, the determination of its objectives, its substantive features and issues. In the selection stage, we decide what we must do, and at what the plan is aimed.

We can list three basic dimensions of the selective (or strategic, or decisional) model:

1. Aims of Utility or Welfare (Final Goals): (Dimension I).
2. Policies or Means (Intermediary Goals): (Dimension II).
3. Territorial Distribution (Spatial Goals): (Dimension III).

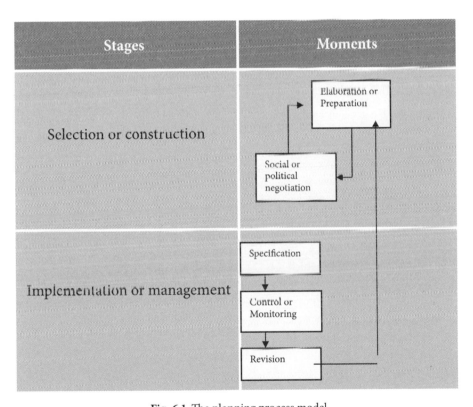

Fig. 6.1. The planning process model

of Britton Harris (1965a, 1965b), J.W. Forrester (1969), W.L.C. Wheaton (1967, 1974), A.G. Wilson (1968, 1974). In their entirety, these modelisations were (in spite of their practical ends) limited by a "positivist" and "interpretative" approach and therefore, in my opinion, they were not and are not as operational as is the model outlined here (in the hope, however, that it could be further articulated and qualified). For a very interesting excursus around Webber's vision of planning theory and on many other stimulating observations, see a contribution by Luciano Vettoretto (1996).

Dimension I, pertaining to aims of utility or welfare, may be articulated through a taxonomy which corresponds to a satisfactory (and conceivably exhaustive) classification of all factors of social or public welfare. Let's imagine such a list as follows:

a. Basic needs
b. Health
c. Public safety and protection
d. Housing and physical environment
e. Social integration and social defence
f. Learning and education
g. Recreation and cultural needs
h. Accessibility
i. Political participation, and so on.

Dimension II, pertaining to policies and means, classifies the various modalities that may be employed to achieve the welfare goals. Such a classification must above all take into account the economic and financial constraints for the achievements of these aims. The dimension's articulation, therefore, may follow the set of policies that aim at achieving the social and public welfare goals expressed in the first dimension:

a. Policy for basic needs assistance
b. Incomes policies
c. Policy of services
d. Health policy
e. Employment policies
f. Transport policies
g. School policies, and so on.

Finally, Dimension III of the selection planning system pertains to the plan's territorial scale and consequent spatial goals. In public planning, various territorial scales may be envisioned within which it is reasonable to measure welfare status, goals, and the effectiveness of policies directed toward particular objectives. Such a list of territorial scales might include:

a. The urban community[27]
b. The national community[28]

---

[27] Personally, I do not believe that the welfare goals can be defined, nor can policy effectiveness be measured at a scale smaller than the "urban system" (whose minimum threshold cannot be smaller (at the present concept and requirement of quality of life) than 500,000 citizens, at least in the advanced Western countries). See also the findings of a European multi-national research directed by me and performed by the European Commission (Archibugi, revision of the Actvill research (1998d), forthcoming). Those who think differently could introduce sub-urban scales.

[28] The sub-national regional scale is largely present in the mind of planners because there exists, in many countries, an intermediary territorial authority between the national country and the urban community. However, in my opinion, these scales would be improper for many measures of social or public welfare (too big for a proper urban public welfare

c. Supranational community (if existing)
d. The planetary cosmopolitan community.

All this is expressed in Fig. 6.2.

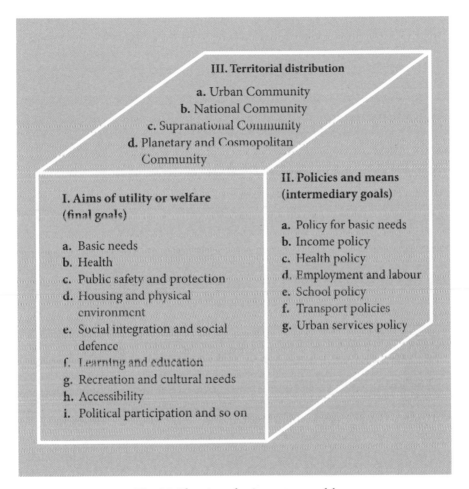

Fig. 6.2. Planning selection system model

and too small for a proper national public welfare) and, consequently, also improper for the implementation of adequate policies. Between the national community and the urban community (in the minimum threshold concept referred to above), I do not find sufficient reason for a meaningful measurement of the quality of life and welfare targets; the eventually existing administrative or political entities should be reduced to the urban system or scale concept. If some peculiar, particularly impacting ethno cultural motivations manifest themselves on a regional scale, people should assimilate this case to the national community case (Archibugi, 'The Ecological City, etc.', 1997).

As stated above, Dimension I is where analyses are made concerning the consistency between, and compatibility of, the various goals in a community of reference. In Dimension II, the analysis compares the degree of consistency and compatibility between the goals and the means at society's disposal for achieving them. More importantly, this dimension also analyzes the economic and financial feasibility of the various means available. To Dimension III belongs the consistency and compatibility analysis of the reference community's plan with the plans of "other" communities in the context, including those of a superior level or scale of territorial representation. (To the last dimension belong all kinds of issues such as the subsidiarity principle, or, more generally, federalism issues).

The relationship between the three dimensions is the means whereby we check and examine the consistency and compatibility between all plans, all related decisions, and between plans and their general decisional context or environment.

6.4.2 The Planning Implementation System

As identified above, implementation is one of the two essential stages of planning (see Fig. 6.1). It is upon this stage that we base the operational articulation of planning, its control of effectiveness and ongoing evaluation, and its political and procedural features and issues.

We decide in the implementation stage how, or by which method, we implement what we have decided to do in the selection stage.

The logical priority of the selection problem over the implementation problem is undeniable. It is appropriate that we act only when we have a reason for our action. Equally undeniable, however, is the fact that we derive from our actions (as feedback) new perspectives on our preferences[29].

As asserted in Postulate No. 3, the subject of planning in the field of public planning is the institution, and the implementation problem includes not only how to do something, but also *who will do what*. Any modelling of the implementation system must take this into account. A successful plan will require a degree of effective co-ordination between the various planning operators, i.e., between the various institutions.

As in the case of the planning selection system (Fig. 6.2), we can describe an operational model or scheme of the implementation system in three basic dimensions (see Fig. 6.3). Such dimensions shadow the decisional or strategic model as follows:

- The policy institutions (governmental institutions and agencies by type of service and/or responsibility): (Dimension I).
- The societal or civil institutions (non-governmental agencies including enterprises, households, and non-profit organizations): (Dimension II).
- The territorial institutions (agencies, governmental and non-governmental, by territorial jurisdiction): (Dimension III).

---

[29] Wider references to this kind of argument can be found in the interesting collection of papers on "social action" edited by Seebass and Tuomela (1985).

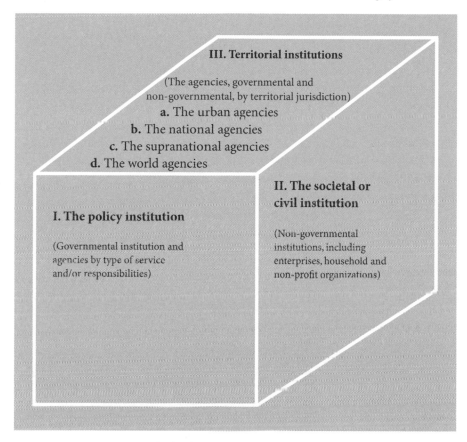

Fig. 6.3. The implementation planning system model

Dimension I, that of policy institutions, includes all governmental agencies that are in some way involved in managing the decisional model's goals, and is, so far as is possible, organised in conformity with Dimension I of the selection model.

The taxonomy of this dimension corresponds to governmental organizational structure (for basic needs, for instance, it would be the welfare agency or ministry; for health, the health policy agency; for accessibility, the transport agency; and so on).

Dimension II, concerning societal or civil institutions, includes all non-governmental institutions whose decisions and actions have a non-negligible impact on the implementation of the strategic model's goals and policies. These may be ranged within the following sub-categories:

– the enterprise system, which operates in the for-profit market and has an over-abundance of effects (both positive and negative) on the strategic model's plans, objectives, and policies;

- the households, the final institution targeted by the majority of plan objectives, that may constitute (at least in the selection of objectives) an important partner of governmental agencies during the formulation of objectives;
- the "third sector" or "non-profit" organizations, which are agencies and operators particularly interested in the implementation of plans and often act as the government's powerful allies in this regard.

Dimension III, finally, concerning the territorial scales and consequent spatial objectives indicated by the strategic model's territorial dimension, includes all agencies, governmental and non-governmental, that operate within a territorial jurisdiction. Among this list are:

a. The urban agencies[30];
b. The national agencies;
c. The supranational agencies;
d. The world agencies.

From this list of the dimensions and their taxonomies we derive the implementation system's actual model (Fig. 6.3).

6.4.3 Functional and Time Interdependencies

The two schemes proposed here provide a framework for, and are intended to stimulate the analysis of, all factors with respect to their consistency and compatibility in: 1) the selection planning process; and 2) the implementation planning process.

In the case of planning's selection process (or formulation process, or preparation process), any preference function (with or without negotiations and agreements between interested parties or stake holders) that is without a contextual framework and devoid of a compatibility analysis of the relevant factors, risks returning a "suboptimal" or precarious decision. In short, such a function is directed towards a very partial and ephemeral optimality.

In the case of the implementation (or management) process of planning, any action undertaken independently by an institution without regard for actions simultaneously undertaken by other institutions in the same environment, is in danger of neutralizing or annulling the plan, and thus constituting a considerable waste of energy and resources (this is the true, unfortunate "story" of several countries' planning in the past decades).

Co-ordination, a task imperative to any type of multi-dimensional management, has the propitious effect of encouraging recognition and evaluation of all factors at stake. Even if it should fail in actual and operational effectiveness, the reference to an implementation framework, as conceived above, would still be useful in shedding

---

[30] In every country the spatial and territorial agencies are, in fact (as said above), for more than just one level and scale (the urban scale, more specifically). This means that the objectives identified in the plans, according to the essential territorial articulation of the strategic model, will be related to agencies and authorities of more than one level (from the local to the national).

light on possible conflicts and could ensure easier decision-making for the operators; it may, in fact, facilitate what could be called "spontaneous" planning[31].

In order to make this co-ordination between institutions effective, however, it is necessary that the content of decisions and choices be co-ordinated, well known, and identified within a comprehensive framework. If this is not done, co-ordination operates in darkness, as an end-in-itself, sterile and, perhaps, even dangerous[32].

It is therefore indispensable to operate a permanent comparison between the two systems, separately conceived, of selection and implementation (see Fig. 6.4). Through this comparison, we can position people to control and monitor the validity of both the strategic or selective planning process, and the implementation and organisational planning process. The ability to move with conscious understanding of cause and effect from one system to another, from one plan to another, or from one scale to another, would immeasurably increase the planning system's quality, so much so that the difficulty of conceiving and implementing a plan, any type of plan, without such means of comparison would become evident and obvious (as it is, in fact, in our current practice)[33].

Given this vision and perspective, we may ask ourselves what sense there is in many of the current discourses on planning (those, for instance, which compare or prefer a "blueprint" method to an "incrementalist" method; a "generalist" (or comprehensive) method to a "case-by-case" method; and so on) that are all questions discussed and "marketed" under the title "planning theory", but that, in reality, de-

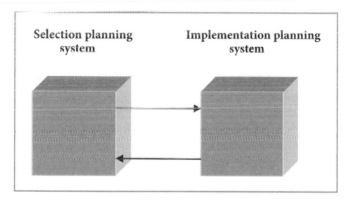

Fig. 6.4. Control of the interactions between the selection planning system and implementation planning system

---

[31] Is this "spontaneous planning" not similar to the idea of a "planning society" which a joint committee (USA Congress and President) outlined in the 1977 report cited above? (US Advisory Committee on National Growth Policy Processes, 1977).

[32] This is what I recommend to Alex Alexander when he analyzes (1993) the functionning of the "inter-organisational' coordination".

[33] In effect this occurs implicitly, without the assurance of an explicit and systematic analysis and without a "check list" of all the interdependencies in play. *Planning theory, for which we argue here, consists in putting in evidence, first of all, this checklist.*

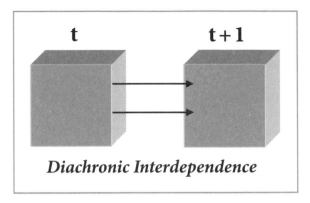

Fig. 6.5. Diachronic conflict between planning systems

rive their existence precisely from the absence of an adequate and appropriate planning theory! Even more distressing from this vision and perspective is the practice of bringing forward as evidence actual cases or life stories (of plans) to support this or that methodological argument. Who doubts that anecdotal evidence might be found to support any particular thesis or method?

Finally, in both planning systems (selection and implementation), it is useful to compare the diachronic states (see Fig. 6.5). Any system is subject to variations over time, which require evaluation in order to avoid when, as in our case, the system is used as a diachronic or taxonomic tool of evaluation, inter-temporal comparisons based on parameters that have themselves changed with time. (This is a very common cognitive mistake that often recurs in the collecting of current data.)

6.5 Conclusions

In conclusion, this "sweeping" picture has sought to provide (as stated in the beginning) only a rapid sketch of what planning theory's occupation should be, in order to be a *true* planning theory. This sketch supports and explains my certain uneasiness, developed in the first chapters of this booklet, about the current trends in planning theory as a whole.

That said, the planning process and system outlined in this paper should be decompressed from its current compactness by a critical analysis. The hypermatrix which springs from the system schemes should be examined cell-by-cell in order to increase our understanding of the interdependencies that are located within.

In this manner, planning theory can make important cognitive advances and provide constructive (rather than destructive) guidance to planning itself.

7

The Future of National Planning Systems: Some New Steps

The planning system outlined in Chap. 6 includes *the national scale* in its dimension III (the spatial), both in the plans selection system (Sect. 6.4.1) and in the plans implementation system (Sect. 6.4.2).

In the plans selection system, the national scale assumes the form of the objectives to be pursued with reference to the social welfare factors (economic goods, health, housing, education, accessibility, and so on). In the plans implementation system, it assumes the form of the actions to carry out in order to achieve those objectives (on behalf of the national institutions).

In this chapter, I will focus particularly on the planning process as it concerns the national scale[1]. And I will discuss what the future of national planning can be, coming from every point of view after some of the experiences that we have had in the previous century.

7.1 The Concept of "National Planning"

In order to talk about the future of national planning, we first need to clarify what we mean by the term. The adjective "national", evidently, delimits planning's *territorial scale* (inclusive, however, of all possible difficulties stemming from the highly variable sizes of different countries)[2]. Even neglecting this objective disparity of references,

---

[1] This was one of the themes with which the Aesop engaged during its XII Congress (Aveiro, Portugal 1998) and, it is opportune to say, this was unusual, in respect of its previous Congresses and also in respect to the prevalence of cultural and scientific interests of its associates of almost all coming from experiences of urban and regional planning.

[2] In Europe it is legitimate to ask what relation can exist between planning at a "national scale", not only of the Granduchy of Luxembourg, but even of spatially and demographically important countries such as the Netherlands, Belgium, Denmark, Greece, and others with that of the scale of countries like France, Germany, Great Britain, and Italy, as well as others whose many regions have a territory or population greater than the "national" countries above (not to mention any comparison with North American countries).

"national" planning can be regarded (and, in fact in the history of the last century, has been regarded) from several viewpoints. We can distinguish at least three major viewpoints:

1. It consists of the use of the term "national" in order to mean the co-ordination by a national government based always on the pivot of town planning policy. Planning remains "town planning," while the guidelines, managerial modalities and rules are elaborated and dictated at a national scale.
2. On the contrary, the term "national" elevates the physical and land use planning, usually applied first at urban and regional levels (master plans and other plan forms), to a national scale, i.e., to the whole territory of a country. In this sense, the prevailing problems are: the greater physical infrastructures; the country's communications and transportation networks; environmental and land use protection issues; interregional and intercity accessibility concerns and so forth.
3. Finally, the term means planning's more general shift from the physical dimension to the socio-economic one, given that, at a national scale, a set of socio-economic issues is emerging, which deserves to be subject to the planning methodology.

Indeed, a rigorous, systemic concept of planning could not admit these different viewpoints, except in a systemic vision that includes the entire domain of planning. Such a vision would consist of many facets belonging to a single prism. It could not admit a disordered application, as is the case today, for the different "substantive" planning experiences that lack any external co-ordination in their plan design and implementation; multiple plans are often overlapping and inconsistent, with heavy damage to their reliability and feasibility.

7.2 National Planning in a Systemic Vision

In a systemic vision, which also belongs to a "rational" vision (to the only possible rational vision) of planning, national planning would unify all three of the above viewpoints. It would try to identify the substantive connections between them and also try to establish the substantive aspects of analysis and decision-making belonging to the national scale itself (in contrast to the other possible scales, for instance: sub-national, supra-national, or global). All this would be done in an integrated vision and approach to planning, including both socio-economic and physical-environmental planning.

Therefore, beyond the actual and historical experiences that could induce us to speak about types of planning completely different from each other (that rarely share common experiences with reciprocal benefit), if we wish to build the foundations for a general and really comprehensive planning methodology (or "planning science", or "planology", as I would prefer), capable of unifying in a common structure or frame all kinds and types of planning, we need a national planning able to find its own place in a multidimensional frame. A national planning so capable would be able to draw and develop its relations with all "other" levels, modes, and varieties of planning, and, if it is admissible that the technical-professional operator of planning, the "planner", be active mainly in one territorial *scale* (urban, regional, national, supra-national) or in one *substantive sector* (land use, transport, industry, environment, etc.), and from this activity draw the best of his or her experience and skill, much less admissible is it that he or she not be prepared (at least in the educational phase of his career) to know how to deal with problems and issues and, overall, *interactions* concerning *all the planning dimensions* (as is unfortunately the present case everywhere in higher education, planning science as an integrated and unified discipline has yet to take shape)[3].

7.3 What Opportunities Exist for the Systemic-Type Development of National Planning?

The prospective of a systemic-type development of national planning is not very clear. The weight of the past is strong. However, even the vision of an uncertain present can provide some possibilities. In any case, the role of the scientific community, and the professional community as well, will be crucial. Although scientific developments and professional applications are normally strongly influenced by political and organisational demands (or, if not this, then by a lack of technical supply), a strong engagement on the part of the scientific and professional communities could provide an effective contribution for more co-ordinated and conscious practices.

7.3.1 The Weight of the Past

It is useful to glance at the different experiences of national planning around the world in the last century, in order to evaluate their meaning and limitations regarding a systemic concept[4].

A first historical example of national planning, it is hard to deny, is the Soviet example of the 1920s, which was essentially a matter of economic planning that was never systemically integrated with physical planning, not least because the Soviet regime was characterised by insufficient political decentralisation. Moreover, the lack of a developed and complex social context, the cultural and technical backwardness, the lack of entrepreneurial capacity, the absence of a free market and free initiative, all deformed the planning experience into a system of bureaucratic enforcement with scant participation.

In the 1930s, the American "New Deal" attempted to introduce similar procedures of national economic planning, supported by a group of qualified economists[5], under the guise of the priority being the best use of national economic resources. But even this national economic planning experience was dissociated from the city-planning experiences which were also developing in that country.

---

[3] Archibugi, 1992

[4] This further survey complements (with some unavoidable repetitions) of that made in Chap. 2.

[5] See, for instance, Wesley Mitchell (1935), G.B. Galloway (1941); the *National Resources Committee* (1935).

It was the post-war recovery in European countries that induced (in the 1940s and 50s and, lastly, in the 60s) several experiences of (macro) economic planning at the national scale. This kind of national planning has been called "indicative" (just to emphasise its radical difference from the Soviet economic planning called "authoritarian"). Even this kind of planning, though, did not introduce an integrated systemic vision, and was developed without any strict relationship with a physical approach at a national scale, and also without any real connection to the regional and urban planning that was in progress at that time in countries such as: (a) France, where the Commissariat au Plan was accompanied by the Datar, that the national delegation attached to the physical and regional development; and (b) the Netherlands, where despite the traditional connection between physical and economic planning at the national scale, favoured also by the country's small size (it is difficult to find even one document of the Central Planning Bureau, even in its best period, in which land use and economic aspects are evaluated in an integrated way[6]).

None of these experiences was sufficient to stand in the way of the demonstrated inadequacy of the (almost exclusively) macroeconomic approaches; nor did they stand against the insufficiency of the effective integration between the macroeconomic planning and the operational structures of the public administration[7].

In Italy, at the beginning of the 1970s, an attempt was made (with the creation of an official body, "Research Institute for Economic Planning", ISPE) to build a complex system of national and regional accounting, inclusive of a social and environmental non-market or informal accounting. This effort was intended as a tool for a very integrated evaluation and management of the country, and for overcoming the conventional and inadequate macroeconomic approach to decision-making and planning at a national scale. The suggested methodology represented a technical advancement beyond the usual planning approaches[8]. However, the implementation of this research was not taken into consideration even by the planning authorities themselves[9].

---

[6] For more information on the problems of disassociation/association between indicative macroeconomic planning and physical planning, see an old report of mine for the UN Centre for Housing, Building and Planning (Archibugi, 1969), prepared for an international seminar in Bucharest.

[7] See an ONU integration report.

[8] The application has been named "Progetto Quadro" (as "Computable Framework for National Programming"), a large research project for the preparation of the 2nd National Plan (1971–75) (see Archibugi 1975, and later, 1993).

[9] It is also irrelevant to remember that the wide experience of the first two United Nations "decades of development" (the 1960s and 1970s) provided the impulse for many (essentially macro-economic) plans at a national level, in many developing countries. This was also a failed experience because of the scant managerial capacities in those countries, and the distorted role of a plan (as in the USSR in all its experiences) by the ruling classes and the dominating regime. Later, attention came to be concentrated on individual projects, mainly funded by Western multilateral or bilateral assistance, without entering into a systemic and operational logic, which, if difficult in the developed countries, would have been more incompatible given the political and managerial immaturity in developing countries.

In the face of these scattered and intermittent experiences of "national" economic planning, in the 1970s and 1980s we also observed some attempts at physical planning at a national scale. The best, in my opinion, has been the experience of the German *Raumordnungsprogramme* (territorial planning programme) (1972–75) designed by the federal Government in co-operation with the *lander* through a common planning committee. This programme has split the whole German territory into about thirty urban-regional "units" (*Gebietseinheiten*), as critical referential entities (not related to the current administrative boundaries), which are only related by the functional role of a "city effect"[10].

More recently (in the 1980s) we observed (under the influence of the environmentalist wave) an interesting experience of environmental national planning in several countries: in sequential order, Japan, the Netherlands, Great Britain, France, Canada, Italy, and others. These long-term plans, for the most part oriented to the physical aspects without co-ordination with the economic implications, have been able to elevate physical issues to a national scale that before were dealt with only at a local scale; and they have contributed, in a certain way, to overcoming the disciplinary isolation of the different scales.

Finally, in the 1990s, national planning was given a strong impetus within many countries by the introduction at the central government level of new management methods and, especially in the USA, of the so-called "strategic planning"[11].

Well, these last innovations of strategic planning at the US federal level have had, in my opinion, a very important impact on the perspectives of national planning. In fact, they are so important that they deserve special consideration.

7.3.2 Strategic Planning at the National Scale

The American federal act of 1993[12], called "the Result Act", introduced for all federal agencies (including the "Departments") the obligation to prepare: 1) strategic plans, that "shall cover a period of not less than five years … and shall be updated and revised at least every three years"; 2) yearly performance plans, "covering each program activ-

---

[10] An extension and updating of both the above quoted Italian and German experiences of physical planning at the national scale (based on the identification of functional and "programmatic" urban systems or city-regions) can be found in a more recent research carried out by the *Planning Studies Centre* on behalf of the European Union Commission (under the co-ordination of F. Archibugi, 1998). Among the findings of this research (related only to four European countries, i.e., France, Germany, Great Britain and Italy), four maps were designed (one for each country) concerning a proposal for a spatial reorganisation of "urban effect" in the national territory; with three kinds of strategies for every urban system identified: "polarisation", "depolarisation" and "rationalisation." For more information see a forthcoming publication; a summary of this research (and these maps in colour) can be found on the PSC Web page: *www.planningstudies.org*

[11] Strategic planning otherwise calls to mind previous attempts to introduce the methods of the "Planning-Programming-Budgeting System" (PPBS) in the 1960s; however, it seems that now the administrative and political commitment is completely different.

[12] *Government Performance and Result Act (GPRA).*

ity set forth in the budget of such agency" (beginning in the first year of the strategic plan); 3) the performance report, concerning the *ex post* evaluation of the performance plan implementation.

Furthermore, the act forecast the future obligation of the agencies to build a *performance budget*, i.e., a budget based on the actions, sequences and results achieved by the performance plans. Program budgeting permits the government and authorised decision-makers, to evaluate *ex ante* (using various *ex post* data) the relative effect of single expenditures in terms of results achieved, and to operate, based on the effectiveness of the various expenditures, a more conscious trade-off between different packages (or scenarios) that use federal resources, with a real knowledge of the efficiency of each expenditure. We will consider later the implications of this new opportunity for the federal governments.

At the moment, it is very interesting to observe how the Result Act outlines (and constrains the program designers to respect) the contents a) of the *strategic plan*; b) of the *performance plan*; and c) of the *performance report*.

The *strategic plan* "*shall contain* (sec. 3/a):

1. a comprehensive mission statement covering the major functions and operation of the agency;
2. general goals and objectives, including outcome-related goals and objectives, for the major functions and operations of the agency;
3. a description of how the goals and objectives are to be achieved, including a description of the operational processes, skill and technology, and the human, capital, information, and other resources required to meet those goals and objectives[13];
4. a description of how the performance goals included in the (performance) plan (next and new sec. 1115 of US Code) shall be related to the general goals and objectives in the strategic plan;
5. an identification of those key factors external to the agency and beyond its control that could significantly affect the achievement of the general goals and objectives; and
6. a description of the program evaluations used in establishing or revising general goals and objectives, with a schedule for future program evaluations".

The *performance plan*, according to the Result Act (sec. 4/a), is requested by the Director of the Office of Management and Budget from each agency every year, "*covering each program activity set forth in the budget of such agency*[14]", and "*such plan shall*:

1. establish performance goals to define the level of performance to be achieved by a program activity;

---

[13] For the purpose of complying with the performance plan, the agency "*may aggregate, disaggregate, or consolidate program activities, except that any aggregation or consolidation may not omit or minimize the significance of any program activity constituting a major function or operation for the agency*" (sec. 4/c).

[14] In sec. 3/c of the Act it is stated that the "*performance plan shall be consistent with the agency's strategic plan*," and that "*a performance plan may not be submitted for a fiscal year not covered by a current strategic plan ...*"

2. express such goals in an objective, quantifiable, and measurable form unless authorized to be in an alternative form under subsection (b)[15];
3. briefly describe the operational process, skill and technology, and the human, capital, information, or other resources required to meet the performance goals;
4. establish performance indicators to be used in measuring or assessing the relevant outputs, service levels, and outcomes of each program activity;
5. provide a basis for comparing actual program results with the established performance goals; and
6. describe the means to be used to verify and validate measured values".

The *Program performance report,* in turn presented[16] by the chief of the agency to the President and the Congress, shall have the following contents:

"*Each Program performance report shall set forth the performance indicators established in the agency performance plan ..., along with the actual program performance achieved compared with the performance goals expressed in the plan for the fiscal year ...*" Furthermore, "*each report shall:*

1. review the success of achieving the performance goals of the fiscal year;
2. evaluate the performance plan for the current fiscal year relative to the performance achieved toward the performance goals in the fiscal year covered by the report;
3. explain and describe where a performance goal has not been met (including when a program activity's performance is determined not to have met the criteria of a successful program activity under (performance plan) or a corresponding level of achievement if another alternative form is used (see note 7), A. why the goal was not met; B. those plans and schedules for achieving the established performance goals; C. if the performance goal is impractical or infeasible, why that is the case and what action is recommended;
4. describe the use and assess the effectiveness in achieving performance goals of any waiver (under the sec. 9703 of this title); and
5. include the summary findings of those program evaluations completed during the fiscal year covered by the report".

7.4 The American Federal Strategic Planning: Its Effects on the National Planning Future

This act, although federal law, and although aimed exclusively at the planning of federal (i.e., governmental) agencies, has a significance and impact as an important act of planning at a national scale that cannot be ignored.

---

[15] In subsection (b) it is established that "*if an agency, in consultation with the Director of the OMB, determines that it is not feasible to express the performance goals for a particular program activity in an objective, quantifiable, and measurable form, the Director of the OMB may authorize an alternative form*". It lays down some further guidelines with respect to the adoption of such "alternative forms".

[16] "*No later than March 31 2000, and no later of each year thereafter*" (new sec. 1116 of the amended *US Code*).

Moreover, the GPRA, or Result Act, has received and brought to a national (federal) scale a multitude of experiences developed in the last 20 years at state and local levels (and also by individual cases from other countries, giving to all this an unsuspicious single pattern of rationality and essentiality), and it is already having a "demonstrative effect" at every sub-federal governmental level. It is a matter of a national movement for planning at the national scale.

It is difficult not to consider such an act, even in its present limited function, an important step toward a national planning system, and it is highly unlikely to have only unimportant demonstrative effects in other advanced countries as well.

The act (which became, as an amendment, an integrated part of the *US Code*), engrafted a process that will be difficult to reverse. September 1997 saw the first important rendezvous for the delivery of all strategic plans from the agencies, and for the plan preparation the act requires that "*the agencies shall consult with the Congress*" (sec. 3/d); to what extent has this consultation been implemented? And what forms has it taken? Perhaps the answers to these questions can be found only case-by-case, i.e., agency by agency. In any event, the work to evaluate the strategic plans which were delivered in September 1997 has already begun (with a kind of score for each plan as determined by a multicriteria analysis and evaluation).

Moreover, the act (by the same sec. 3/d) prescribed that when developing its strategic plan, the agency "*shall solicit and consider the views and suggestions of those entities potentially affected by or interested in such a plan*". Evidently, these entities are those groups commonly called in recent political jargon, the "stakeholders".

Even if the act does not explicitly call for an "*inter-agency*" type of consultation and co-operation (i.e., between different units of the federal government), in fact the start of intense reflection and programming activity has represented a significant development in this direction. The same is also true at an *inter-governmental* level (i.e., within that country between the federal government and other local and state governments); in the directions of assuring consistency of objectives and resources employed and of obtaining possible synergies, important developments have occurred.

This is the reason why the act cannot (especially with its increasing implementation) avoid producing a national planning movement, involving sectors outside the strict control of the federal government.

All this is in order to obtain the necessary evaluation of the federal government's program activities, to evaluate the federal programs' direct and indirect effects (positive and negative) on the entire social system of the country.

7.5 From Strategic Planning to National Economic Programming: A Necessary Step Towards Systemic Planning

The great and growing weight of the public sector in any advanced country, in terms of the State's income and expenditure as a proportion of the GNP, and with respect to the whole societal context, is such that we cannot imagine a governmental expenditure planning without an evaluation of its effect on the economic system as a whole, and therefore without a comprehensive planning vision of this system.

Already, the strategic planning for every program activity and every performance budget must be evaluated with respect to its effect on the entire societal context, beginning with its "target" population, or beneficiaries, and it is impossible that a selection and evaluation process of individual expenditures in the performance budgeting, could not be aggregated into a public budget at the national level, in order to evaluate its effectiveness, priority preference, compatibility, and necessary alternatives and options. We know, too, that this unavoidable assumption at the national budgetary scale cannot also avoid a comprehensive evaluation of the effects at the scale of the entire societal context.

The problem, and it is a big problem, is that this process, required by the evolution of strategic planning's innovations at the governmental scale, has found, to date, neither the political consciousness necessary for its operational implementation nor even the technical consciousness on the part of the scientific and professional community of planners required for its conceptual and technical implementation[17].

7.6 Toward a Scientific and Professional Approach to the Systemic Planning

What I mean to say here is that the scientific and didactic community shows itself today to be terribly unprepared to provide valid tools of knowledge and of professional skills to this emerging type of strategic planning at a national scale, and to give attention to the unavoidable connections it is making towards a more comprehensive system of societal planning (including its socio-economic and environmental components).

My opinion is that, independently from the historical appointments with the willingness and implementational practices of the strategic planning, and accepting the risk of an approach that could be too "rationalist" (as many are only too ready to point out) and disappointing in its results, the scientific community has the duty to prepare (with all didactic implications about the know-how), the interpretative and conceptual schemes of a *multi-dimensional, multi-objective, multi disciplinary,* and *multi level* planning. Where, of course, the emergent "national" scale could again find its full role, its effectiveness and its dignity, (even to the benefit, in this systemic consciousness, of "other" effective and feasible planning, at other scales).

And the scientific community has the duty to work consistently in this direction. To improve the conceptualisation and the methodologies, simulating the implementations according to the nature of the planning approach: to pursue not *what is* but *what should be:* and this without despairing that the evolution of things and the general improvement of the consciousness could also influence the practical or political implementation of this general planning above outlined.

The Aesop Congress (1998) has already set the theme of the "future of national planning systems" as an important one at or for this period. It is imperative to give,

---

[17] A more in-depth discussion can be found in (Archibugi 2005a and b).

year-by-year, a positive answer to that Congress's invitation. It is to be hoped that the future will be marked by an intensive study and research in the direction of the relationship between strategic planning and multi-level and multi-agency systemic planning, of which the scientific community (especially that which occupies itself with "planning theory") should be able to outline not only the existence but also the functioning.

8

Planning and Plan Evaluation:
Some Well-Known and Often Neglected Pitfalls

In this book, we have seen the *approaches*, the *first routes*, the *thematisms*, for a re-evaluation of planning theory and methodology as a tool for the modern governance of public affairs. It is a matter of first approach, aimed at fixing some "boundaries" within which the planning theory can be re-founded as, in my opinion, a safer and more effective development.

However, let me close this essay with some final considerations concerning some of the risks or pitfalls which are often inherent to the evaluation and planning processes.

The clever reader can easily perceive that these pitfalls are most dangerous when, within the logical framework outlined in Chap. 6, a clear vision is lost, along with the systemic link to the framework itself (and what the framework implicates as information and evaluation). The correct use of the above mentioned framework already constitutes, by itself, a security against the evoked risks

However, it is appropriate to accompany the discussion of an integrated vision of planning and its methods with a rapid treatment of those risks that are always lurking behind any partial and sectoral application.

These pitfalls and traps are normally very neglected or forgotten in the usual evaluation and planning practices; and this has been a cause not least of that crisis of planning discussed in Chap. 1. They have damaged not only the results of evaluation, but also the credibility and reliability both of evaluation and, ultimately, of planning itself.

These pitfalls to which I refer, and which are all logically inter-related, as we will see, could be named as follows:

1. logical indeterminateness;
2. systemic disconnectedness;
3. strategic insubordination;
4. self-referencing;
5. sub-optimization;
6. bounded rationality.

In this chapter, I intend to highlight some of the negative consequences produced by the existence of such pitfalls, and the negligence of them; and to discuss how a conscious management of evaluation and planning, if practiced, can help to extend in a suitable way the planning practices[1]. This extension depends, on the one hand, on the removal of the pitfalls themselves and, on the other, on the development of a "true" planning science (or planology), the development of which is the object of this book.

8.1 Logical Indeterminateness: "Evaluation" vs "Values"

The first pitfall to which I wish to draw attention, that of *logical indeterminateness*, occurs when people state that the evaluation process could be exempt from values, or "value-free". This creates a series of misunderstandings that deserve to be discussed and enlightened upon.

It is usual, in any evaluation process, to state that the contents of the evaluation pertains to some "values" that, in turn, correspond to some "value-judgements" and by which the evaluation itself cannot help but be influenced.

As is well known, this statement is present in the methodological reflection of political economy. It has founded, in its own time and in its own way, the logical "priority" of the "value" respecting the "evaluation," either to state or research the "technical" *independence* and *neutrality* of the evaluations from values[2], or to declare the *impossibility* of such independence and neutrality[3].

In other words, a great, principal stream of economic thinking[4] (made up of numerous strands) has sought to assert that the concept of "value" in the evaluation that concerns us is typically (and implicitly) "economic"; and that the behaviour of individuals, groups, and communities is ruled by an *axiomatic logic of utility which explains the behaviour itself* (and, therefore, studies and codifies it) leaving out the substantive *values that determine such utility*. An extreme example: *utility* for one person could be to acquire commodities, and for another person utility would be to donate them, but both "utilities" (or choices or preferences) coming from different values, could be subject to the same behavioural rule, for instance the "decreasing marginal utility" rule concerning the commodities[5]. Therefore, these rules are the proper realm of the economic science, whatever the goods/commodities exchanged might be.

---

[1] For more considerations on this topic, I suggest the recent collection of papers edited by E.R. Alexander (2006) in honour of Nathaniel Lichfield, and also another earlier paper by E.R. Alexander (1998b).

[2] Economic thinking itself, from the very beginning, has aimed towards a "value-free" assessment, but the author who comes to mind above any other, for the specificity of the subject, is Lionel Robbins (1935).

[3] In the same way, economic research has always faced challengers of not only the possibility but even the unavoidability of a value free assessment and the author who comes to mind above any other for the vastness of his engagement with the subject is Gunnar Myrdal (1953, 1958, 1972).

[4] As is well known, this stream is usually defined (by its opponents) as *main*, i.e., "mainstream", dominant and, maybe a little ironically, "orthodox".

[5] According to which: the more the pleasure or need becomes satisfied, the more the utility of this good (and therefore its value) declines. In such cases orthodoxy does not hesitate to assert: if individuals aim to acquire the *good-wealth*, the value of the wealth declines with the

Another important stream[6] (which is made up of more numerous individual strands than the "main stream") contests the possibility for an economic theory to leave out certain value premises from its formulations: but nothing dramatic! It is sufficient for this stream *to make values explicit*, and a good deal of its economic reflection or findings can be equally well grounded, but on the logical constraint of the assumed premises, and provided that they are not presented as "natural" and "objective" facts (in the way of natural sciences), independent from historico-institutional conditioning.

However, as stated, both the opposing schools of thought have one thing in common: both consider value (neutral or implicit) as a basis for evaluation.

Even in the more confined area of the planning theorists, and of the plan evaluators, it is usual to start from the presupposition that evaluation cannot do anything but:

1. Either, *leave out of consideration all values* that preside over decision-makers' choices, and confine planners to the presentation of "analyses of facts" or "technical evaluations", which allow the decision-makers to make decisions on the grounds of whichever values they choose to pursue (this should implicate the effort to build evaluation methods which could be "neutral" respecting the values).
2. Or, on the contrary, urge decision makers "to make their values clearly explicit" (in terms of goals) and, on the basis of these goals, to construct the very same evaluation process; in such a case, the planner and/or the evaluator could find themselves being much less neutral, but strong partisans to the point of almost assuming the role of co-decision makers.

Both routes, starting from the analogous presupposition (*evaluation depends on the values*), involve two risks:

- of constructing a biased evaluation, without being aware of it (in the first case);
- of supplying partisan evaluations, which could limit the prerogatives of the decision-makers (in the second case).

It seems to me that both risks have been well perceived. For instance, Nathaniel Lichfield, with his usual clarity, states:

> ... a tidy distinction can be maintained between the politician's values and the planner's facts. But whereas it is important in practice constantly to have in mind distinctions between fact, value and value judgement, it is very difficult to avoid overlap in

---

growth of the wealth. But I am not sure that the same happens, according to their assertion, if in the place of the *good-wealth,* we introduce other goods of which individuals can feel the utility (pleasure or need): *good-solidarity, good-power, good-respect* (of themselves), *good-rectitude, good-affection, good-sociality, good-wisdom, good-success,* among others. Walter Isard, (1969) consistently with the logic of the neo-classical approach, called these goods "commodities," i.e., subjects of exchange.

[6] This stream is generically named as "heterodox" and we have the feeling that this qualification is not unwelcome by interested people. We all know that in economics different words have been used to oppose this stream to the "mainstream": "historical school" (namely in Germany, in the 19th century) or "institutional economics" (like in the USA during the last century), or "evolutionary school" (everywhere after the Second World War). More insight can be found in Hodgson (1988).

practice. Politicians become aware of the substance of the planning and evaluation process and cannot be constrained in exercising their views; and even where the professional respects the prerogative of the politician on deciding on values, he cannot but reflect his own values in the professional contribution; in a sense he is arguing for a modification of values in the decision-making when he urges a change in decision through demonstrating the opportunity cost of the politician's inclinations. Since there is not homogeneity in planner's values, the argument for change will be diverse. Furthermore, the dialogue on these lines tends to modify the stance of each, as they *progressively work* over time through the planning and evaluation process (Lichfield, CIE, pp. 198–199, italics mine).

Lichfield thinks, then, that the two risks can be avoided in the planning process when, as we proceed "progressively," the politicians modify their "stances" (we might also say, this could be the great educational function of the evaluation process, mainly if it adopts the CIE method).

But doesn't this change of stance suggest also a different stance towards values in the planning process? Or a different concept: i.e., a concept that could allow us to overcome the possibility of the above stated risks?

We have seen, up to now, that in an approach of "positivist" analysis, the choices (and preparatory evaluation) are developed on the grounds of values, based on the assumption: *evaluation depends on values.*

But in a programming (or planning or planological) approach, which is a *decisional* approach i.e., a decision-oriented, or action-oriented approach, should we not overturn the assumptions, and should we not test what would happen if we began from the assumption that: *values depend on evaluation?*

At this point, it would be useful to come back briefly to the foundations of a "theory of value," on which entire generations of scholars, not only of economists, have been engaged and disputing[7].

In fact, to evaluate means to assign value to something, and it is hard to avoid posing the question, in order to be sufficiently critical: what is meant by "the value"?

It has been said, and generally accepted, that "value" is a property of things, but one which is different from, say, their colour or weight. The value of a thing is substantially derived from its ability to satisfy need or desire. The greater this ability, the greater the value. However, and this is the first step for a reconsideration of how the value is posed on the basis of the evaluation, the value is not a fixed and inherent property of the thing. It's rather a variable property, the magnitude of which depends not only on the nature of the thing in itself, but also on whoever evaluates it and on the circumstances under which it is evaluated.

In summary, I think there can be different values according to different goals, in different moments, for different persons, under different conditions (for instance, the physical environment within which the evaluator is working), and in general terms

---

[7] Here I rescue the reader from exhaustive references. I note only a book which has been very useful to me as a compendium of the different positions regarding the problem, the book by Hutchinson (1964). For the analysis of the concept of values I have profited largely from K. Baier (1969) and other essays from Baier and Rescher (1969).

under the different circumstances (personal, physical, psychological, social and political) of the evaluator, either political or professional, in the moment in which he evaluates[8].

This being the case, why don't we ask ourselves: if the value is a variable property, how can it be at the base of the evaluation, and thus be a guide to the decision?

The answer is not hard to find if we base it on another important assumption: that decisions and evaluations are never general and universal, nor could they be. They always represent limited choices and evaluations which seem to be the best solution in respect of the problems that they face (in the so called "problem solving" approach). In other words, human problems tend to be specific and the decisions that concern them must also be specific. I think that this principle of evaluative specificity must never be forgotten.

Therefore, if the value doesn't exist by itself, but only because of the utility that it provides (or the needs and pleasures which it satisfies) even this utility exists in that, and in that moment, it is evaluated as such. Neither value nor utility exists without evaluation; moreover, they exist only at the moment of evaluation.

And, whereas we are dealing with a *decision-oriented* evaluation (and not with an evaluation *tout court*), for our purposes the values also acquire concreteness only in the context of a decision. Even when we obtain general consensus about them (and in political life, at general level, such consensus can be obtained easily) people only truly appreciate the values of things and of actions in peculiar circumstances and situations, when these values can be compared with their practical feasibility and implementation; and this limits their capacity to "value" as such.

And, whereas values can be appreciated concretely only in the course of the decisional process, their validity depends strongly on the process itself.

In conclusion, how good the value can be as a guide to decisions depends strongly not on the value in itself but on the circumstances and the ways in which decisions are taken.

All this puts us in the face of the *overturning* of a dominant paradigm, and of a new appropriate approach to the evaluation: it is not the evaluation that depends on the values, but, rather, the values that depend on the evaluation.

This recuperates the independence of the evaluation process from the trap of a subordination to values, which is in turn translated into an indeterminateness of values themselves. In fact, it is not a matter of having to choose between values, but to assess between alternative decisions, taken from stances that may be different according to different circumstances.

This occurs through a re-visitation of the distinction, always required, between the role of the politicians (decision-makers) and the role of the technicians of planning (planners). This distinction operates in a new way; it's not a matter of politicians,

---

[8] We can get a non-conventional vision of the variability of the values in a classical work by Charles Morris (1956). In this work the problems are discussed in a masterly way: of scales and dimensions of values; of the different determinants of the value, from that social, to that psychological and biological; and the meeting between the Western and the Eastern values (which are often neglected) are also discussed.

as porters of the power of decision, and technicians, as porters of the power of suggestion. The values, pre-existent or not, in generic and/or ideological terms, *emerge in fact only within the evaluation process*, of which technicians (planners) are the designers and operational "guardians", and politicians are the main actors (if you will, having in the scenario negotiation and partnership with the stakeholders)[9]. As the process perfects itself and assumes a more complex importance, the values take the form of their natural trade-off achieving a kind of "optimality".

It is rather a matter of a permanent interweaving between politician and planner in the evaluation of this kind of optimality.

8.2 Systemic Disconnectedness

Another pitfall is also strictly related to the logical indeterminateness, well represented by the examined relationship between values and evaluations: we have named it "systemic disconnectedness".

This disconnectedness is produced when, in an evaluation process (taking the dependency on the values of the evaluation at face value, and forgetting the more intimate interweaving between evaluation and "formation of values"), people assume that to be able to base the evaluation on the assumption of certain values[10] without such values having been "incorporated" in a previous or parallel evaluation process.

The "system" of values applied in the previous (level) or parallel (sectorial) evaluation process, and the resulting trade-off obtained in the research of the optimality in that process, can be different from the system of actual processed values. The diversity of the two (or more) value systems, acknowledged by neither of the evaluation processes, can create situations of remarkable inconsistencies between the decisions to which such processes have lead at these two (or more) levels or sectors. This could be considered a lack of systemic interconnection of these two (or more) evaluation processes.

Of course the same lack of inter-connection could occur, not only between the two levels or sectors of evaluation and planning, but also between two environments, two time periods, two issues which can be integrated in some way and for some reason in a system, and the same can be said of the *n*environments, time periods, sectors and issues of which any defined social community is composed.

It is necessary therefore, to try to *interconnect the systems* in order to make more explicit not only the values but also the evaluative criteria adopted at different scales or sectors of application; and it is necessary also that we not ignore the need to respect some hierarchical criteria either logical or institutional, if it is the case and if it is possible.

---

[9] At this moment, the participation modality is not the subject of this consideration.

[10] If you will, expressed on the spur-of-the-moment by decision-makers, maybe in a political document of guidelines or general preferences. The well-known work of George Chadwick (1971) is a milestone in this analysis.

8.3 Strategic Insubordination

All of the above can be presented from another point of view under the guise of another pitfall of the evaluation: that of the lack of a "strategic consistency" between the goals and objectives that are assumed as evaluational criteria. Whereas, in the planological and systematic approach[11], the value depends on the evaluations and not the other way around; we need to affirm a certain "hierarchy" between evaluations and between the criteria that are used in any evaluation process.

Therefore, it is strongly recommended that any evaluation process, instead of arriving at the end of the road at a conflict (which would mean falling afoul of the pitfalls of the "strategic insubordination", as in reality the planning practices are right now), should co-ordinate its own hypothesis on the strategic consistency with the other possible hierarchical superior levels (or, at least to make such a hypothesis explicit, made by itself for the superior level).

The more decision-makers and planners show awareness and willingness to avoid the risk of strategic insubordination, the more they contribute to the general need to create networks of strategic planning. Within this network, when developed, some conflicts of jurisdiction and/or interest will inevitably exercise their negative roles; but through it the progress of knowledge and of a system of *learning by doing* could also have some unsuspected positive effects[12].

Certainly, if we could create a national and international planning system, institutionally well established, strategic consistency could be strongly facilitated[13]. Through such a system we could be induced to elaborate some guidelines in which the fields and the strategic jurisdictional entitlement for each of the scales and levels of decision-making should be better described; in such a way even the scale and level could also be more easily defined; and more appropriateness could be found for the definition of the criteria/objectives of every imaginable evaluation process.

In the absence of such a system, and of related deontological rules, something of this kind has been attempted with what has been called "subsidiary principle", to regulate in abstract the relationship between different hierarchical levels; moreover to give a ratio to the specification and creation of the hierarchical levels themselves.

To carry out something of this nature could be considered the task of methodological thinking (in this field we are very backward), exactly as "planning science"

---

[11] Again I refer to the basic work of George Chadwick (1971) to get broader information on this approach. At that time Chadwick based, on the contribution of Lichfield, his view on the relationship between evaluation and system approach (see Chap. 11). Other insights on this topic are in some papers included in an other edited book by Lichfield (1998); like the papers by A. Barbanente, Batty, Borri, Breheny & Hooper, Glasser, and Khakee.

[12] It is a commonplace to state that modern information technologies are ready to facilitate these strategic planning networks. In the past I have studied functional relationships between information technology and planning, and complained that information systems have not been designed with rigorous adherence to the processing of a strategic planning framework, but only a generic planning database (see for a beginning of this framework, Archibugi 1978 and 1993).

[13] For more details on this topic see another paper of mine (Archibugi 1998c).

(or planology). (This could be one of the more useful and significant issues in order to characterize the proper field of planology).

The strategic planning experiences especially ongoing in the great and significant season of strategic planning within the American Federal Administration, inaugurated in 1993 by the "Government Performance and Result Act" (GPRA), and its implementation (of which we have spoken in Chap. 7), will be able to provide a very important contribution for defining ways and means of increasing this form of strategic co-operation in the planning field, and of creating a sort of planning system. All this would prevent planners from having to wait for the reforms of the political institutions in order to enter into an improved rational conception of public governance and to elaborate such a conception.

Something could be made from the application of theoretical reasoning to some concrete political cases, on behalf of the planner's and evaluator's scientific community. For instance: in fixing the evaluation rules and criteria, what are the boundaries between what the object of individual preferences could be, and what, instead, the object of community or public preferences must be? And, to remain in the ambit of community or public preferences, what could the margins of autonomy be regarding community preferences according to different levels of sociality, territory, and public administration?

Whereas the evaluation cannot be disassociated, in a correctly conceived planning system, from the objective's preliminary formulation, and cannot help but depend on the evaluation process itself, rather than on the general ideologies[14], the study of how a strategic evaluation system should be articulated by hierarchical levels will become, more and more, co-essential to an effective development of planning. How can the planner's scientific community neglect making this possible articulation one of its subjects of research, and then of didactic?

The lack of strategic connection gives way to another pitfall of the evaluation: that of self-referencing.

8.4 Self-Referencing

Self-referencing is another insidious pitfall of evaluation. More than a pitfall, it is an endemic disease of evaluation based on the unequal development assumed by practices of evaluation in respect to that of systemic planning.

Self-referencing occurs when the results, performances, or effectiveness, of a plan, program, or design, are evaluated without assessment parameters derived from plans, programs, or designs of a scale and level superior in a program structure.

Self-referencing represents the consequence of the lack of logical consistency. Free from any of the constraints of superior planning, which define performance objectives and goals, the plan evaluator accepts the parameters of assessment established by the plan itself, at face value, or he suggests them himself. This is common behaviour in the majority of plan evaluation experiences that have been implemented everywhere

---

[14] Which become more and more generic as the societal planning techniques progress.

in the history of evaluation. The lack of a more systemic network of multi-level and multi-sector planning, planners and plan evaluators have been reduced, in order to develop evaluation in limited terms, to the planning unit concerned or committing the (professional) task. This is what I call *self-referencing evaluation*.

In the best case, with the lack of sufficient constraints to use as parameters, conscious planners and plan evaluators have found a way to *simulate* by themselves those necessary constraints coming from other levels or sectors. But in this case, surely more advanced and required from a rational point of view, they have, on the contrary, created a circumstance in which, on one hand, conflicting situations are easily avoided but, on the other hand, the evaluation has been rather a mystification and the final result, from an operational or implementational point of view, has usually been a disaster.

Yet all the great seasons of the evaluation-without-planning have been marked by a diffused prevailing self-referencing evaluation, more or less effective at the micro level but without sense at a more general level, and for this reason no trace of this evaluation has been left behind[15].

The diffusion (syndrome) of the self-referencing evaluation has created a circumstance in which we are hardly able to perceive the tautologicality of certain evaluations, or certain absurdities[16].

These attempts from the history of evaluation seem to have had very poor success. Moreover, they seem to be well known as failure stories, and their abandonment, or their application only at a much reduced scale, without any emphasis, seems to suggest an effort to improve performance only in the ambit of micro-designing.

Indeed, this is a mistake. These experiences were wrong only in their approach to evaluation, and they have discouraged their progressive enlargement. It is only by this enlargement itself, however, that we could have improved the context in which they could be more effective and more significant in the future.

In fact, what we have called self-referencing evaluation can be contrasted by applying as far as possible its opposite: the *hetero-referencing*. This means finding where possible external references on which to base the ongoing evaluations.

All this brings us back to the need either of the systemic interconnection or of strategic consistency aforementioned.

---

[15] These seasons, for instance, have been those of the "cost-benefit analysis" of the project, especially in development policies in the developing countries (on behalf of the World Bank and other United Nations agencies); and those of the "environmental impact assessment," launched after 1970 in every country, not to speak of many other projects born out of the developing policies in every country, in an effort to carry out developing sectorial and/or territorial policies.

[16] Which reminds me of the tale of Baron Von Munchausen, who tried to save himself from the river into which he was falling by holding onto himself by his hair.

8.5 Sub-Optimization

Sub-optimization is, in effect, the comprehensive result to which the lack of systemic connection, of hierarchical consistency, and so on, leads to the usual evaluation processes regardless of which technique is being employed.

Because an optimization process will never be obtained under optimal rational conditions, and because even under the best conditions that we could forecast (on the basis of the peroration of the previous paragraphs: better or improved systemic connection, hierarchical consistency, and so on) a system will never achieve the perfection striven for, our intellectual honesty impels us to acknowledge, obviously, that even sub-optimization is a permanent or continuous characteristic of any planning or evaluation result.

However, such acknowledgement and assertion, to be expected at a superior critical level (meta-critical), for nothing must affect the research of an improved optimality at operational level. The very risk in the abandonment of awareness regarding the need of a systemic connection, hierarchical consistency, and so on, is to effectively abandon the research into optimality in more advanced possible frontiers. Therefore, the pitfall is not in the awareness of the limits of rationality, but rather in the abandonment of rationality itself, only because we have discovered its limit!

This impels us to examine how, from a planological viewpoint, the generally accepted theorem of bounded rationality, is not only "limited" in its heuristic validity, but is also absolutely useless from the operational point of view. Moreover, it can constitute another general pitfall of planning, through the suggestion (as is unfortunately the case) of the abandonment of the rational approach to planning.

8.6 Bounded Rationality

For the most part, the meaning of the bounded rationality concept is born out of, as is well known, the ascertainment that, in any decision, there are always limitations or boundaries of time (in decision-making), of resources, of information, of intellectual capabilities, and so on. Obviously this warrants the conclusion that decision-making is always bound by something.

However, in this assertion another implicit belief is also incorporated: if there were no limitations, the decision could be "rational" or "optimal"; in practice this decision could be "not bounded". What could we call it? A "pure", perfect decision, exempt from limitation?

At this point, however, we must ask ourselves: is there (in the life of people, in their values, in their actions, in their thinking) anything that isn't *bounded*? Everywhere man or man's society, in every decision as in all thinking, will be limited in his striving for rationality. But what does all this tell us against the rationality of which they become permanently "searchers" or "porters", according to the cases? And what does this obvious fact tell us against the other assertion: that they should be in any way searchers and porters of such rationality?

Even the purest mathematical theorem is subject to the same knowledge limitation, by definition: if it weren't for some further knowledge progression of the mathematics itself from which it has spread!

Imagine if we didn't take for granted the idea that much of the modelling that we elaborate in order to understand (and also in order to manage the reality of things in certain ways, or in order to give sense to our actions), was the product of a bounded rationality! But if the rationality is bound by itself, there is no need to introduce the bounded rationality as a limitation of rationality itself.

On the other hand, in what way should or could our limited knowledge limit the search for knowledge itself? Would this mean, perhaps, that knowing the limitations of every human action in respect of goodness, we should not try to be good? Or, knowing the limitation of any aesthetic expression, should we not research the beautiful?

Indeed, research of the optimum or maximum (or minimum) "constraint", which is also maximum given the limitations, includes the consciousness of the limitations, and it would be of little use to say that we will never know entirely these limitations and, therefore, any optimum will never be a true optimum, an absolute optimum, but will always be relative to the limitations that we have been able to take into account *pro tempore*. All this doesn't exempt us from the intellectual opportunity or duty to research that optimum, that maximum (or minimum) given the limitations (obviously acknowledged). Nor does all this exempt us from the intellectual utility and task for a deeper understanding of most of the limitations that we don't know, in order to make the research of this optimum more valid and significant.

Therefore, rather than emphasizing the obvious, i.e., that our rationale is limited, (not, it seems to me, having any heuristic value) should we not limit ourselves to looking deeply, I would say case by case, into whatever thing any proposition proposed to us in the name of rationality, is actually limited by conditions or constraints that are not included in the calculus? That is, should we not limit ourselves to look deeply into what the output of the rational calculus has been, rather than at the level of the rationality that was pretended?

In other words, it seems to me that rationality, in its concrete manifestations or applications, can be contested only in the name of a "superior" rationality. But from this, it follows that this superior rationality must be demonstrated by including new limitations in the calculus, ignored from the proposition that we intend to contest; and not in the name of something alternative, of general value, which does not exist, if not in an act of antirational faith: i.e., in the name of an anti-rationality philosophy or irrationalism[17].

Thus, while it is not possible to deny rationality through rational arguments, it is in the same way not possible to attribute to research into rationality the negative

---

[17] In spite of this, we need to acknowledge that this "fight against reason" and these "crepuscular" and obscure moments of the history of ideas have studded the entire history of human philosophy that we know, and the history of any civilised manifestation of mankind. But it is not my intention here to go beyond a certain "limit" in discussion of the dichotomic and dialectical destiny of philosophy.

results of a bad application of rationality. It is only in the name of rationality that we can identify and contest its insufficient applications.

The vision here illustrated allows us to locate in the right dimension the limited role of the positive analysis in *strategic planning* and in the *programming approach*.

In effect, the reflection and the "science" of administrative and political behaviour can argue any kind of limitation on possible rational theorems of administration and political action only from a position of *ex-post* analysis. Indeed, only in an *ex-post* analysis is it possible to evaluate how much an administrative or political action *has been* limited (or constrained or conditioned), which would pursue a rational principle of conduct. In fact, it is only by an *ex-post* analysis (say historical) that it is possible to identify those "new" conditions or constraints that have had a negative impact on the implementation, and limited the success, of this action. But can we be sure that what have been registered as unforeseen factors in the past can be extrapolated for the future?

On the contrary[18], in a programming approach, what could be meant for the planner (planning theorist or the decision-maker) by a bounded rationality? I have already mentioned the curious attitude of a planner following the bounded rationality principle: "*My preferred solution would be this (A), but I choose, or I suggest this other (B), which is not the best but of which I am equally satisfied; why? Don't ask me because I don't know[19]*". Indeed, if he knew, he would have been obliged to include the reason for this fact in the list of the objectives that he pursues, and within the trade off (i.e., optimization procedure) between different objectives that any decision unavoidably involves.

As already said in Chap. 6, it is possible that, in practice, decision-makers could be unconsciously unconscious, or ignorant, of his preferences; but that he could be consciously unconscious of them is something that concerns maybe psychiatry, not even behavioural psychology!

Here, the more general doubt can be introduced, on that which we can call a "positivist" pretension of an important part of the political and social sciences: can we elaborate some conduct principles or suggestions on the basis of a historical, ex-post evaluation of examined past behaviour, assumed as an orientation principle for a future action[20]?

We know, obviously (and with great emphasis from the political and administration scientists), that the most rational decisions are always limited by an ignorance co-efficient (or knowledge and information limitation): so what can we extract from an *ex-post* analysis for an *ex-ante* decision? Would it not be better to leave out *ex-post* analysis (of little significance for the future) and go *directly* to elaborate not the rules but decisions themselves, on the basis of a decisional process that could be the

---

[18] I have already argued this in Chap. 6 (and I acknowledge in this case the same phrases, because sometimes *repetita juvant*).

[19] How much more exhilarating it would have been if he answered: "*Why? Because Professor Simon said that usually the decision-makers like me think of satisfying and not optimising their preferences*"!

[20] There is a certain amount of literature on this topic; my preferred references are still Tinbergen (1971a, 1971b), Leontief (1976), Frisch (1976), and Myrdal (1973).

most rational possible: i.e., including (according to our vision above) the maximum number possible of constraints, conditions, acknowledgeable limitations, given the circumstances, not received in the past but valid for the future?

This is the true "programming approach" inherited from Ragnar Frisch and the other founders of the planning methodology[21].

If we must talk of rules or guidelines, would it not be better if these were taken from the decisional process itself, trying to make it as far as possible well informed and technically advanced?

Would it not be better, considering the future, if the decision and its process, (rather than explore the field of past behaviour of groups, communities, cultures etc. trying to assume it as a stable "theory"), were based, on the contrary, on an evaluation of explored possible future behaviour, expressly studied or even only hypothesized[22]? And would it not be better that the decision and its process, oriented in such a way, be active as a factor affecting those behaviours?

To conclude, I think that according to this vision the strategic planning doesn't need a "theory of the political and administrative behaviour" but simply (if you will) of a "planning theory": a theory, however, only pragmatic, operational and decision-oriented, meaning that it is oriented to the improvement of the rationality of the decisions and to an operational efficiency under every historical, geographical and cultural condition[23].

Strategic planning therefore, as operational in the field of organisations, and more so in the field of public organisations, if understood correctly, represents a pillar, the main pillar perhaps, of that "planning science" (or planology) which is emerging as the confluence of a series of inter-disciplinary or trans-disciplinary fields of studies and which, I believe, directs us towards the constitution of a new discipline[24], of basic importance for public management and governance at any level, geographical or territorial.

From this vision also comes the overcoming of any theory of bounded rationality and a recuperation of the postulate that: *an analysis- or a decision- or action-oriented analysis is fundamentally optimality-oriented.*

If the analysis is oriented to the action (*ex-ante*), and not to the nature of things observed more or less (*ex* post), any limitations fall outside any limitation respecting decisional objective: it cannot do anything other than to plan and achieve the *best re-*

---

[21] More detail on this topic in Archibugi (2000b).

[22] This future behaviour of groups, stakeholders and politicians, which could constitute the real limit to the rationality of the process, should be the object of the planning negotiations, but on the basis of an advanced systemic knowledge of the optimal decisions.

[23] Naturally, as far as political and administrative sciences abandon the "objective" behavioural analysis approach (which we have defined as "positivist") and adopt, on the contrary, a "programming approach", decision-oriented, or functional to decision, then the roots of strategic planning on those sciences can be fully recognised, and they lose any need for demarcation of it. Moreover, it could be stated that strategic planning can identify itself in those political and administrative sciences, and they can identify themselves in it.

[24] See Archibugi (1992, 1996). See also Chap. 9 of the already cited *Introduction to Strategic Planning* (Italian ed. 2005a; English: in preparation).

sult respecting the objectives, given the constraints[25]. The limitations are incorporated in planning's optimal decision.

That this "best result", in the *ex-post* reality, given the limitations could not have occurred, or occurred in a limited way, has no importance for the planning theorist. This can concern the analysis of *temporis acti,* not the analysis of *temporis agendi*: It could concern the historian, or the historian of planning, or the kind of planning theorist that is not interested in creating new rational methods to improve planning, but only in making a commentary of the mistakes of the past. But it could not concern the *planner*, the real planner theorist (or *planologist*). Nor, on the other side, could it interest or limit the *decision-maker*[26] itself, for whom mere past experience could be a misleading counsellor, if not accompanied by a scientific imagination for the future.

---

[25] For this postulate, see Chap. 6.

[26] For further considerations on my part, regarding the double-separated routes open to the planning theorist community, see Archibugi (1998a).

9

Conclusions

9.1 A question of Prepositions

I hope, at the end of this book, that the reader has perceived what I have intended as the main objective of this writing: to trace the way, the course for a passage, from reflections *on* planning (which has for the last 20 years abusively been called "planning theory"), toward a reconstruction of matters and of operational capacity, i.e., that which should be a true theory *of* planning[1].

This passage can be summarized (as in the subtitle); "from the policy debate to the methodological reconstruction".

It is at the beginning of this writing, specifically at the beginning of Chap. 1, that we have discussed (with reference to the pioneering work of Andreas Faludi and to its game of prepositions) the meaning of this, and the reasons why it is "necessary".

In the first place, the debate I called *on* planning, has induced to unduly extend the field, the terrain of planning itself, and dissolved the object of planning theory in more general arguments of political culture, which have since gained the upper hand.

In fact, from one angle, this debate has become centred on its "traditions", its cultural roots, and its philosophical foundations, with an unjustified extension of its origin, which has made planning the heir of almost all the ideas of mankind (at least those expressed by the so-called "Western civilization")[2]. It is a suggestive hypothesis, one especially gratifying for the actual professional planners (those that are associated in the various academic and professional associations, national and international, of the "planning schools" and the town-planners), but it is also a little egocentric. Many

---

[1] Here the reference is explicitly to the game of prepositions introduced by Faludi (1973a), and already mentioned in Chap. 1. That game of prepositions makes me suspicious that Faludi, since the beginning of the use of the expression, "theory of planning"- in the early 1970s, had already perceived the risk of its misunderstanding, and chosen to wilfully ignore it. This doubt has been formulated by others (for instance, Seni 1996b).

[2] I suspect that this extension of the cultural history of the West is limited, more by the scale and the diffusion of knowledge still existent in the cultivated classes of the West concerning the foundation of eastern culture, than from any substantive choice.

other actual professions have founded their origins in those same ideas, in the names of the same key authors, in those same "historical" turns. So what? What identity can planning find from these origins? It is not by rummaging through the bric-a-brac of tradition that we will be able to know what it must become in the future; all remains yet to be built.

From another angle, that debate *on* planning has become a debate about the primary principle of political philosophy, transforming planning into an object of political philosophy and as, more recently, people believe that they can assert, of "political science," according to the already consolidated and positivistic economical and social "sciences". In such a way, the debate (named "theory") on planning has been reduced to a policy-science debate. Furthermore, there is a special trend towards discussing and elaborating a kind of "psychology" of the behaviour of the main subjects or operators of planning, policy- and decision-makers, of any range and degree, beneficiaries and stake-holders, professional planners, and especially practitioners.

The planning, intended as such, so extensively without an *ubi consistam*, its "theory", the "planning theory", has become essentially a discourse (only abusively named "theory") *on* planning. In this way, it has lost its technical, innovative, and progressive content.

In fact, expanded in its historical-cultural terrain, and in its interdisciplinary recognition, planning theory has withdrawn into itself, engaging merely in self-discussion and, effectively, in little more than self-contemplation.

Planning theory has not perceived that planning, the true one, is yet to be born. To use an expression perhaps improper but effective, I will say that – instead the questions "what must we do?" and "how must it be done?" – people seem to have preferred to answer the idle, even banal questions: "who are we?" and "from whence do we come?".

9.2 A Question of "Adjectivization"

A second wrong-headed approach that planning theorists have taken is that of characterizing the discipline with a specific approach, alternative by definition to some other approach. This reference is not to the traditionally different fields in which people have tried to plan, ground that has been covered above in Chap. 3: *physical* (urban and regional), *macro-economic, social-environmental, developmental* and *operational* planning.

By contrast, I have in mind those methodological approaches that Faludi has already made the object of his basic book on planning theory, defining them as dialectically contrasting modalities, by couple:

1. the blueprint mode vs. the processual mode of planning;
2. the rational-comprehensive mode vs. the disjointed-incrementalist mode;
3. the normative mode vs. the functional mode.

An extended analysis on this point must be left to Faludi, who dedicates a chapter of his book to each of these modalities: Chapters 7, 8, and 9. According to Faludi, there are six modes that are presented as dyadic pairs, each of which has been assigned the concept and the name "planning dimensions"[3].

Therefore, this coupling leads me to the conclusion that he has never intended these modes as distinct, separated approaches, or, worse, alternatives to one another. It may mean that he intends that each mode, and through it each dimension, should be a permanent component or aspect of the same planning process; that any valid planning theory must include them together, without any exclusion.

Faludi says, "In the pure form, (the modes) represent planning at the dimensional extremes, the observable situation falls always in some point intermediately between the two (ibid. p. 131)".

However, to the modes and the dimensions of planning that Faludi had collected in the literature by the 1970s, and which have allowed him to build the initial systematization of the matter into something quite useful and stimulating methodologically to the field, have been added new modes and approaches (even on other levels and viewpoints) which cannot be easily counterposed as extremes like Faludi's set. These new modes tend to give a distinct, separate character to each modality of planning. In such a way have been created what are often called, in the history of ideas, different "schools of thought" or "paradigms"[4].

Frankly, I would not be able to assert in general (nor would this be the place to do so) whether these schools of thought have a positive or negative effect on the progression of ideas and of the sciences. As one who loves and esteems the dialectical process in the development of logical thinking, I would be inclined to say that, in general, the schools of thought play a positive role in the development of the human sciences.

But here, surely, I prefer to argue that in the specific field of planning, many of these approaches or methodological modes: a) turn away from their antonyms; b) each separates from what it intends to deny; and c) being not intended as opposite "moments" of an unitary process of planning, or parts of a research oriented to promote increasingly effective planning, they have lost any sense, and have predisposed planning by its starting point to its partiality, to its unilaterality, to its narrow-mindedness, and, with all this, to its failure and its ineffectuality.

Thus the debate has been consolidated (sold as "planning theory"), tending to counterpose different approaches, each one having the propensity to exclude the other, resulting in a kind of methodological brawl in which it is difficult for me to see any reason, conceptual or practical.

In fact, each mode taken by itself is imperfect if it is not integrated with the others. This is because single "adjectivizations", when they tend to exclude each other, have

---

[3] The reference to Faludi's work doesn't mean that a legion of other taxonomies have been proposed after Faludi (see, for instance, B.M. Hudson 1979, and "his heuristic rubric of SITAR: Synoptic, Incremental, Transactive, Advocacy, Radical schools of planning thought"). Much of it has been examined by Faludi himself in his further answering to the comments on his work (Faludi 1987).

[4] I will leave the argument to a good reading of the papers presented to a famous seminar on philosophy of science held in London in 1965 (with contributions by Kuhn, Popper, Lakatos, and others, edited by Lakatos and Musgrave 1970).

a nefarious effect on planning method's progress and, consequently, on its potentially best effect.

Exceptions are those "adjectivizations" that claim the completeness and compresence of the approaches; among the most used: *comprehensive, integrated, unified,* and also *systemic.* These are adjectivizations, at least in their intentions, wish to give a holistic meaning to planning, but even the other adjectivizations, which intend to express not a specific, substantive field of planning, but just an approach, should be used only when we have to emphasize one aspect of the prism that has been considered peculiarly neglected in didactic writing, or in such a processed and proposed plan or practised plan. But not, however, for the reason that any one of these approaches should be considered hegemonic with respect to the others.

9.3 The "Rational" Approach Case and the "Communicative" or "Collaborative" One

One of the most recent "adjectivizations" is the *rationalist* (or modern?) one versus the *communicative* (or post-modern?) one[5].

Some reasons are well known: the difficulty in carrying on the operations of "blueprint" plans, according to the criteria of mere rationality, has induced difficulty in discussion and diminished the prospect of other ways to carry out plans. The possibility is impugned, for instance, of deriving plans from intense analysis and debating among the multiple policy-makers, a possibility that holds real promise, especially if we start from the remark that in modern political societies, decision-making is a fact so evident and "real" that it cannot be neglected without some elements of foolish irrationality[6].

In effect, to combine participation, collaboration, and bargaining into a concept of planning, by means of a sharpening of the available information and the communicative procedures of all the stake-holders, and particularly of those who can play a specific role in the implementation of plans, has been rightly stated as the central factor of planning itself[7].

Such a mistake arises when we begin to think that any one of the participative, or collaborative, or communicative, or bargaining approaches should be so important as to become a special *way*, or a *kind*, of making plans, alternative to other ways or kinds, thereby neglecting *other* essential factors of planning development that are equally important. Such essential factors include the capacity to elaborate serious, responsible calculations of compatibility between objectives, calculations of optimal resources used, calculations of consistency between decisions and resources, etc.

---

[5] I don't wish to enter in the question of modernism and post-modernism in planning, which I consider another idle question. Anyway, I suggest reading on this subject: David Harvey (1989), Goodchild (1990), Albrecht and Denayer (2000) and Allmendiger (2001).

[6] See Alexander (quoted, 1998a). See also John Forester (1993).

[7] See the emphasis given to this point on behalf of certain authors: John Forester (1996, 1999); Patsy Healy (1992, 1997); J.E. Innes (1995).

All this leads to reasoning in terms of modes, types of methods and approaches to planning, different from each other, in which every type of mode, method, or approach becomes privileged, and is considered the decisive solution for planning's effectiveness.

The apperception of this mistake must not induce in the reader, however, the misconception that I intend to argue that any way or type of planning implementation could be acceptable, could have its own sphere of influence and validation, its right to exist and to be developed without being criticised or defined as "wrong". This would be a "Pollyannaesque" and overly tolerant interpretation of planning theory, which could also be termed "possibilist" (whereby all is possible, acceptable, valid). This attitude often masks a critical incapacity that, despite its ostensible openness, entails, rather, a substantial intolerance only toward critical capacity and intelligence (which have been the main motors of intellectual progress).

I do not intend to argue this here. Instead, the intention is exactly the opposite, that *any* single mode or type of planning, taken by itself, and exalted above each of the other possible modes as *the* mode *par excellence*, the one which allows the plan to achieve results, to not fail, to achieve objectives, to be simply implemented, etc. is fallacious; I argue that it is improper and misleading to require any such "turn"[8].

In the continuous, dialectical process of knowledge construction, there are surely some paradigmatic "turns" which constitute a radical overthrow of the dominant way of thinking. This aspect has always been present in the evolution of philosophical thinking and commented on by its historians[9]. But in the planning evolution in its different aspects and disciplinary fields, which have been briefly summarized in Chap. 3, it doesn't seem to me that there is space for such a "paradigmatic" revolution. It seems to me, rather, that "planning science" needs (or would benefit from the attempt) to aim at a more integrative methodology. This may well resuscitate the moribund condition of the discipline, fractured as it stands (or falls) now by partial, disjointed, and fragmentary approaches that talk past each other instead of fostering real progress. "Planning science" needs to continuously perfect its methods (and to better implement techniques that are currently poorly applied) in order to strive with less superficiality and more professionalism, toward planning operations.

The discipline needs to extend the "scope" of its visual field, to be more mindful of the limits and conditions imposed by "new" factors (called "substantive") which must be taken into account in the planning process. This would mean true progress in planning science, and lead to more optimal decision-making.

In order to do all this, we need to not abandon too easily old ways of planning, because of their respective incompleteness; otherwise we risk throwing out the baby (which must be fed and fortified) with the bathwater.

There is no substitute for an intuitive, preferred or sponsored approach; there is only the need to integrate it with the other in a polyhedral and prismatic way.

---

[8] See Fisher and Forester (1993) and Albrecht and Denayer (2000).

[9] Presently in the more restrained court of the social sciences, the most frequent (and perhaps exaggerated) reference is made to the treatment developed by Thomas S. Kuhn (1962).

9.4 The Diagonal of "Planology"

The diagrammatic scheme of Fig. 9.1 can help us to summarize the essential method-ological message of this writing, towards an ameliorative and positive evolution of planning as science, as "doctrine" if you will, and as implementation.

The horizontal axis displays the various aspects or disciplinary fields (marked by capital letters) of planning that have succeeded in the past century (which registered planning as having been born and developed as a managerial method of public deci-sion and intervention). Out of necessity, we will indicate these in a historical, chrono-logical progression (very questionable): 1) first the *physical* planning, which, it seems to me in order of time, has preceded the others (at the end of the 19th and the begin-ning of the 20th centuries); 2) later, the *macroeconomic* planning, which had its main result in the management of scarce resources (especially in war-time), 3) still later, *socio-environmental* planning, by multiple strands aimed essentially at the integration of an economic vision with varieties of issues that have been formerly neglected, such as social and institutional constraints to action, the distribution of opportunities, the power of groups and classes, the formation and the diffusion of local, social initiatives, and the evaluation of issues concerning natural conservation, especially concerning non-renewable resources; 4) later still, the *development* planning, aimed at the solu-tion of under-developed programs; and finally, 5) *operational* planning, arisen from systems-analysis and engineering and from operational research, and developed into strategic planning first in the corporations, and then in public administration[10].

The vertical axis displays various approaches to planning that are discussed presently in the debates called "planning theory", and prevalently in the field of phys-ical planning or of the planning of territorial units, though this debate is not absent from the other fields as well.

From this cross section comes a series of typologies of encounters and bilateral crossings, each represented by a cell of the matrix, and of multilateral crossings rep-resented by more of these cells put together.

The development line of a planning science (or "theory"), for which I would like to propose the name "planology", is of continually integrating more cells; defining for each such aggregation, the object, the methods, the application techniques, and the experiences.

This tendential development line, however, could not be other than that *diagonal* which tries to integrate all cells, of all fields and of all approaches, in an organic system, defining the system's contours, limits, and methods. This could be the constructive work of a true "planning theory", or of the "planology".

It is a work that remains entirely to be done, even if some of the constructive elements are already available[11].

In Chap. 6, I have proposed the model on which it could be possible to achieve the collection of the highest possible number of cells. The final purpose should be

---

[10] These fields of planning have been briefly illustrated in Chap. 3.
[11] More than simple allusions to all this are in: Rittel and Webber (1973); Webber (1978); Al-brecht (1992); Scheele (1982); Alexander (1993); Farago (2004).

Fields \ Approach	1.Phisical Planology of territorial units	2.Macro-economic Planology	3.Socio-environmental Planology	4.Development Planology (DC)	5. Operational Systemic Planology	Systemic interrelation
A. Blue-print vs. Processual Planology	A-1	A-2	A-3	A-4	A-5	A-Ω
B. Functional vs. Normative Planology	B-1	B-2	B-3	B-4	B-5	B-Ω
C. Rational-comprehensive vs. Disjoint-Incrementalist Planology	C-1	C-2	C-3	C-4	C-5	C-Ω
D. Strategic Planology	D-1	D-2	D-3	D-4	D-5	D-Ω
E. Negotiated-communicative Planology	E-1	E-2	E-3	E-4	E-5	E-Ω
Σ Global synthesis	Σ-1	Σ-2	Σ-3	Σ-4	Σ-5	Σ-Ω

Fig. 9.1. The diagonal of planning

to apprehend and consolidate at last the conception of the cell Σ Ω (see e.g., Fig. 9.1 which represents graphically the final regime of all methodologies of systemic planning, the corpus of notions, references, new operational fields for all planners, and of a didactics aimed at educating them technically and professionally).

To commence a discussion amongst the scientific and professional community concerning other models would itself constitute progress, so long as this discussion would conclude with the intention to perfect and standardize a model akin to the concept contained in the Σ-Ω cell. The diagonal represents exactly such a progressive effort, necessarily slow, of integrating fields and approaches, given starting points that are several and different, and that are suitable for the most varied occasions and practises of integration.

The multiplicity of approaches and of fields to be integrated would not miss the mark. It would jettison, on the contrary, the lack of consciousness and the ingenuity needed to operate in different fields, with different approaches, without a clear vision of the interdependencies that can emerge from the multiplicity of approaches and fields. This, rather, ought to be the role played by a planning science or "planology", which would be indispensable and provide a propaedeutical basis for different implementations and applications in the numerous fields of substantive planning[12].

To conclude this writing, I would like to say in brief that, of all the experiences that can be derived from the multiplicity of approaches and from the multiplicity of the fields to be integrated, some are useful and meaningful and some are not. These different types must not be pitted against each other.

The failures and successes in our plans (as in our lives) are never absolute, never total. Even when people feel the need to turn the page, this always comes with something acquired, earned. The only problem is to choose the faster path, and to pursue it with firmness, a firmness that flows from an ethical commitment and a clarity of ideas.

As I had the occasion to say, in a polemical writing of mine that inveighed against an experience of "blueprint" urban planning[13], the main impediment we face is the belief that just using some labels such as "structural", "strategic", "systemic", "integrative", (some time ago we discovered also "negotiated", "communicated", "participated", and others) can characterise truly different schools of thought in the planning field. On the contrary, I have the firm conviction that planning must always be at the same time: structural, strategic, systemic, integrated, communicated, participated, negotiated, multipurpose, and so on; otherwise *it is not planning*, or at least, it is a planning subject to grave limitations of meaning, of completeness, of implementability, and of results.

If we could all consent on this point, then it would be possible for all people to operate for the improvement of what has formerly been called a "planning science", or "planology". That discipline, in other words, which is suitable for preparing planners (without other adjectives) to take into account the polyhedricity of planning, and its multiple aspects, even if only procedural; in order to be better prepared to operate in specific fields (those defined "substantive"), in full consciousness of the systemic, strategic, and structural interconnections of each individual field with all of the others, none excluded.

---

[12] The work of Laslo Farago (2004) – it seems to me – is developed in the same length wave.

[13] In Chap. 7 of a book on *Rome: a new planning strategy* published by Routledge (London: 2005b), dedicated to a critical comment on the new master plan of Rome (2002).

Bibliographical References

Ackoff RL (1962) Scientific Method: Optimizing Applied Research Decision. Wiley, New York

Ackoff RL (1974) Redesigning the Future: A System Approach to Societal Problems. Wiley, New York

Albrecht L (1992) Dilemmas in Planning: What is and What Ought to be. First-World-Wide Conference on Planning Science, Palermo, September 1992

Albrecht L, Denayer W (2000) Communicative Planning, Emancipatory Politics and Postmodernism. In: Paddison R (ed) Handbook of Urban Studies. Sage, London, pp 369–384

Alexander ER (1986) Approaches to Planning: Introducing Current Planning Theories, Concepts and Issues. Gordon and Breach, New York

Alexander ER (1993) Interorganizational Coordination: Theory and Practice. J Plan Lit 7(4):328–343

Alexander ER (1998a) Rationality Revisited: Planning Paradigms in a Post-postmodernist Perspective. Planning Theory Conference, Oxford Brookes University, School of Planning, 2–4 April

Alexander ER (1998b) Conclusions: Where do we go from here? Evaluation in Spatial Planning in the Post-modern Future. In: Lichfield N et al (eds) Evaluation in Planning: Facing the Challenge of Complexity. Kluwer Academic Press, Dordrecht

Alexander ER (ed) (2006) Evaluation in Planning. Evolution and Prospects. Aldershot (England, GB), Ashgate

Allmendinger P (2001) Planning in Postmodern Times. Routledge, London

Allmendinger P (2002) Planning Theory. Palgrave Macmillan, New York

Alonso W (1971) Beyond the Inter-Disciplinary Approach to Planning. J Am Inst Plan 37

Archibugi F (1969) Strategy of National Development and Its Implications for Physical Planning, (Background report prepared for the United Nations Centre for Housing, Building and Planning and presented to the Interregional Seminar on Physical Planning for Urban, Regional and National Development), Bucharest, 22 Sept–7 Oct, 1969

Archibugi F (1974) A System of Models for the National Long-Term Planning Process. Report to a UN Economic Commission for Europe Seminar on the theme. On the Use of a System of Models in Planning, Moscow, December, 1974

Archibugi F (1975) Un Quadro contabile per la programmazione nazionale. Ministero del Bilancio e della Programmazione Economica, Roma

Archibugi F (1978) Les instruments comptables et institutionnels d'une véritable planification sociale, Rapport présenté au Colloque du Comité Planification et Prospective, Institut International des Sciences Administratives, Sousse, 16–19 Mai 1978, Centro di studi e piani economici, Roma

Archibugi F (1980) Principi di pianificazione regionale. Franco Angeli, Milano

Archibugi F (1982) Ends and Means: New Policy Instruments for Social Development, Report to the Conference Out of Crisis. Paris, July 1982

Archibugi F (1985) The Possibilities for Employment Creation in the Third Sector. Report to the OECD Intergovernmental Conference on Employment Growth and Structural Change, Paris, 6–8 February, 1984

Archibugi F (1989) Comprehensive Social Assessment: An Essential Instrument for Environmental Policy-Making. In: Archibugi F, Nijkamp P (ed) Economy and Ecology: Towards Sustainable Development. Kluwer, Dordrecht

Archibugi F (1992) Introduction to Planology. Towards a meta-disciplinary convergence of planning sciences. Planning Studies Centre (first draft), Rome

Archibugi F (1993) The Configuration of a System of Models as an Instrument for the Comprehensive Management of the Economy. XII International Input-Output Conference, Seville

Archibugi F (1994a) The Disciplinary Implications of Environmental Planning and Evaluation. In: Voogd H (ed) Issues in Environmental Planning. Pion, London, pp 164–175

Archibugi Franco et al. (1994b) The Future of Urban Quality in Europe: Towards a New European Urban Systems Concept and Strategy (Draft). Rome, Planning Studies Centre (forthcoming new edition)

Archibugi F (1995) Theory of Urbanistics: Lectures on a Reappraisal of City Planning Methodology (forthcoming in English). Draft. Planning Studies Centre, Rome

Archibugi F (1996) Toward a New Discipline of Planning. Socio-Economic Planning Sciences, vol 30, no 2

Archibugi F (1997) The Ecological City and the City Effect. Ashgate, London

Archibugi F (1998a) Planning Theory: Reconstruction or Requiem of Planning? Planning Theory Conference, 2–4 April, 1998. Oxford Brookes University, Oxford Brookes University School of Planning

Archibugi F (1998b) Planning Theory: Postulate and its True Realm. Presented to the Planning Theory Conference, Oxford, 2–4 April, 1998

Archibugi F (1998c) The Future of National Planning System Planning. Presented to the XII Aesop Congress, Aveiro, 22–25 July, 1998

Archibugi F (1998d) The Future of Urban Quality in Europe. Towards a new European urban systems concept and strategy (based on the results of the research Actvill), (draft) DPC, Rome [forthcoming final publication]

Archibugi F (1999) L'approccio programmatico: considerazioni di metodologia basate su i contributi di Frisch, Tinbergen e Leontief. In: Acocella N et al. (ed) Saggi di politica economica (in onore di Federico Caffè), Franco Angeli, Milano

Archibugi F (2000a) The Associative Economy: Insights Beyond Welfare State and into Post Capitalism Planning. Macmillan, London

Archibugi F (2000b) The Programming Approach: Methodological Considerations based on the Contributions by Frisch, Tinbergen and Leontief. Presented to the Eaepe Congress 2000, Berlin

Archibugi Franco (2005a) Introduzione alla pianificazione strategica, Alinea Editrice, Firenze

Archibugi F (2005b) Compendio di programmazione strategica per le pubbliche amministrazioni. Alinea Editrice, Firenze

Archibugi F (2005c) Rome: A new planning strategy. Routledge, London

Archibugi F, Delors J, Holland S (1978) Planning for Development. In: Holland S (ed) Beyond Capitalist Planning. Blackwell, Oxford

Arrow KJ (1951) Social Choice and Individual Values. Yale University Press, New Haven

Arrow KJ, Raynaud H (1986) Social Choice and Multicriterion Decision-Making. MIT Press, Cambridge

Baier K (1969) What is Value? An Analysis of the Concept. In: Baier K, Rescher N (ed) Values and the Future. Free Press, New York

Baier K, Rescher N (1969) Values and the Future. Free Press, London

Banfield EC (1959) Ends and Means in Planning. In: Int Social Sci J XI, n 3, Unesco

Banfield EC, Wilson JQ (1963) City politics. Harvard University Press, Cambridge

Barbanente A et al (1998) Dealing with Environmental Conflicts in Evaluation: Cognitive Complexity and Scale Problems. In: Lichfield N et al (eds) Evaluation in Planning: Facing the Challenge of Complexity. Kluwer Academic Press, Dordrecht

Batty M (1998) Evaluation in the digital age. In: Lichfield N et al (eds) Evaluation in Planning: Facing the Challenge of Complexity. Kluwer Academic Press, Dordrecht

Baumol W (1961) Economic Theory and Operations Analysis. Prentice Hall, Englewood Cliffs, New York

Beauregard RA (1992) Institutional Constraints and Sub-National Planning: Economic Development in the US. First World Conference on Planning Sciences, Palermo, September 1992

Bellman RE (1957) Dynamic Programming. University of Princeton Press, New Jersey

Benli ÖS (2004) The Current State of Planning: How Plans Get Made. California State University, Long Beach

Berlin I (1964) Rationality of Value Judgements. In: Friederich CJ (ed) Rational Decision. Atherton, New York

Benveniste G (1987) Professionalizing the Organization: Reducing Bureaucracy to Enhance Effectiveness. Jossey-Bass, San Francisco

Borri D (1998) Linking practice to theory. In: Lichfield N et al (eds) Evaluation in Planning: Facing the Challenge of Complexity. Kluwer Academic Press, Dordrecht

Breheny M, Hooper A (ed) (1985) Rationality in Planning. Critical Essays on the Role of Rationality in Urban and Regional Planning. Pion, London

Buchanan JM (1967) The Demand and Supply of Public Goods. Rand McNally, Skokie

Buchanan JM, Tullock G (1962) The Calculus of Consent. University of Michigan Press, Ann Arbor

Burchell RW, Sternlieb G (ed) (1978) Planning Theory in the 1980s: A Search for Future Directions. New Brunswick, New York, Center for Urban Policy Research, Rutgers University

Campbell S, Fenstein SS (ed) (2003) Readings in Planning Theory. Blackwell, Oxford

Catanese JA, Steiss WA (1970) Systemic Planning: Theory and Application. Heath Lexington Books, Lexington

Chadwick G (1971) A System View of Planning: Towards a Theory of the Urban and Regional Planning Process. Pergamon, Oxford

Checkland PB (1981) System Thinking, System Practice. Wiley, New York

Checkland PB (1984) Rethinking a Systems Approach. In: Tomlinson R, Kiss I (eds) Rethinking the Process of Operational Research and Systems Analysis. Pergamon, Oxford

Churchman CW (1961) Prediction and Optimal Decisions. Prentice Hall, Englewood Cliffs, New York

Churchman CW (1968) The System Approach. Delta Book, New York

Churchman CW (1971) The Design of Inquiring Systems: Basic Concepts of Systems and Organization. Basic Books, New York

Cooke P (1983) Theories of Planning & Spatial Development. Hutchinson, London

Dantzig GB (1957) The Shortest Route Problem. Oper Res 5:266–277

Dennis N (1970) People and Planning. Faber and Faber, London

Dennis N (1972) Public Participation and Planners' Blight. Faber and Faber, London

Dewey J (1944) Theory of Valuation. University of Chicago Press, Chicago

Dimitriou B et al (1972) The Systems Views of Planning. Working Paper n 9, Department of Town Planning. Oxford Polytechnic, Oxford

Dorfman R, Samuelson PA, Solow RM (1958) Linear Programming and Economic Analysis. McGraw-Hill, New York

Drewnowski J (1970) A Planning Model for Social Development. In: UNRISD, Studies in the Methodology of Social Planning, Geneva

Drewnowski J (1974) On Measuring and Planning the Quality of Life. Mouton, The Hague

Dror Y (1968) Public Policy-Making Reexamined. Transaction Books, New Brunswick

Dror Y (1971a) Design for Policy Sciences. Elsevier, Amsterdam

Dror Y (1971b) Ventures in Policy Sciences Concepts and Applications. North-Holland, Amsterdam

Dror Y (1987) Governability, Participation and Social Aspects of Planning. CEPAL Review, n 31, pp 95–105. United Nations, Economic Commission for Latin America and Caribbean

Dyckman JW (1966) Social planning, social planners and planned society. J Am Inst Plan 32(2):66–76

Dyckman WJ (1969) The Practical Uses of Planning Theory. J Am Inst Plan (35):300

Dyckman JW (1970) Social Planning in the American Democracy. In: Erber E (ed) Urban Planning in Transition. Grossman, New York

Economic Council of Japan (1973) Measuring Net National Welfare of Japan, NNW Measurement Committee, Tokyo

Etzioni A (1968) The Active Society: A Theory on Societal and Political Process. Free Press, New York

Etzioni A (1969) Indicators of the Capacities for Societal Guidance. St. Martin's. Press, New York

Faber M, Seers D (1972) The Crisis in Planning (Vol. 1: The Issues, Vol. 2: The Experiences). Chatto & Windus for Sussex University Press, London

Faludi A (1971) Towards a Three-Dimensional Model of Planning Behaviour. Environment and Planning 3(3):253–266

Faludi A (1973a) Planning Theory. Pergamon Press, Oxford

Faludi A (ed) (1973b) A Reader in Planning Theory. Pergamon Press, Oxford

Faludi A (1978) Essays on Planning Theory and Education. Pergamon Press, Oxford

Faludi A (1986) Critical Rationalism and Planning Methodology. Pion, London

Faludi A (1987) A Decision-Centered View of Environmental Planning. Pergamon, Oxford

Faludi A (1989) Planning According to the Scientific Conception of the World: The Work of Otto Neurath. Environ Plan 7

Farago L (2004) The General Theory of Public (Spatial) Planning. The Social Technique for Creating the Future. Pecs, Centre for Regional Studies of Hungarian Academy of Sciences

Farkas J (1984) Change in the Paradigms of Systems Analysis. In: Tomlinson R, Kiss I (ed) Rethinking the Process of Operational Research and Systems Analysis. Pergamon Press, Oxford

Fisher F, Forester J (ed) (1993) The Argumentative Turn in Policy Analysis. UCL Press, London

Foley DL (1964) An Approach to Metropolitan Spatial Structure. In: Webber MM (ed) Explorations into Urban Structure. University of Pennsylvania Press, Philadelphia

Forester J (1993) Critical Theory, Public Policy and Planning Practice. State University of New York Press, Albany

Forester J (1996) Planning in the face of conflict. In: Le Gates RT, Stout F (ed) The City Reader. Routledge, London

Forester J (1999) The Deliberative Practitioner: Encouraging Participatory Planning Processes. MIT Press, Cambridge

Forrester JW (1969) Urban Dynamics. MIT Press, Cambridge

Fox KA et al (1966) The Theory of Quantitative Economic Policy. North-Holland, Amsterdam

Fox KA (1974) Social Indicators and Social Theory: Elements of an Operational System. Wiley, New York

Fox KA (1985) Social System Accounts. Linking Social and Economic Indicators Through Tangible Behaviour Settings. Reidel, Dordrecht

Fox KA, Gosh S (1981) A Behaviour Setting Approach to Social Accounts Combining Concepts and Data from Ecological, Psychology, Economics, and Studies of Time Use. In: Juster JT, Land KC (eds) Social Accounting Systems. Academic Press, New York

Fox KA, Miles DG (ed) (1983) Systems Economic: Concepts, Models and Multidisciplinary Perspectives. Iowa State University Press, Ames

Friedmann J (1973) Integration of Economic and Physical Planning. Paper for a Seminar of the Center for Housing, Building and Planning, United Nations, New York

Friedmann J (1987) Planning in the Public Domain: From Knowledge to Action. Princeton University Press, Princeton

Friend JK, Jessop WN (1969) Local Government and Strategic Choice. Tavistock Publ., London

Friend JK et al (1974) Public Planning, The Inter-corporate Dimension. Tavistock Publ., London

Frisch R (1962) Preface to the Oslo Channel Model. A Survey of Types of Economic Forecasting and Programming. In: Geary RC (ed) Europe Future in Figures, vol 1. North-Holland, Amsterdam

Frisch R (1964) An Implementation System for Optimal National Economic Planning Without Detailed Quantity Fixation from a Central Authority. In: Lang F (ed) Economic Planning Studies. Reidel, Dordrecht

Frisch R (1970) Cooperation Between Politicians and Econometricians of the Formalization of Political References. In: Frisch Economic Planning Studies (Lang F ed) Reidel, Dordrecht

Frisch R (1971) An Implementation System for Optimal National Economic Planning without Detailed Quantity Fixation from a Central Authority. In: Frisch Economic Planning Studies (Lang F ed) Reidel, Dordrecht

Frisch R (1976) Economic Planning Studies. (Lang F ed), Reidel, Dordrecht

Galloway GB (1941) Planning for America. H. Holt & Co, New York

Geddes P (1915) Cities in Evolution. Williams & Norgate, Edinburgh

Glasser H (1998) On the evaluation of 'wicked problems': Guidelines for integrating qualitative and quantitative factors in environmental policy analysis. In: Lichfield N et al (eds) Evaluation in Planning: Facing the Challenge of Complexity. Kluwer Academic Press, Dordrecht

Goodchild B (1990) Planning and the Modern/Postmodern Debate. Town Planning Rev 61:119–137 (April 1990)

Goodman R (1973) After Planners. MIT Press, Cambridge

Gottinger WH (1983) Coping with Complexity: Perspectives for Economics, Management and Social Sciences. Reidel, Dordrecht

Hall P (1992³) Urban and Regional Planning. London, Routledge

Hall P (1996) Cities of the Future: Managing Social Transformations. International Social Science Journal (UNESCO) 48(150)

Hall P (1996) The City of Theory. (from: Cities of tomorrow: An intellectual history of urban planning and design in the twentieth century.). In: LeGates TR, Stout F (eds) The City Reader. Routledge, London

Hall P (1996) Revisiting the Non-place Urban Realm: Have We Come Full Circle? International Planning Studies 1(1)

Hall P (1997) Modelling the post-industrial city. Futures 29(4/5):311–322

Harvey D (1989) The condition of Postmodernity: An Enquiry into the Origin of Cultural Change. Blackwell, London

Harris B (1965a) Organizing the Use of Model in Metropolitan Planning. California State Office of Planning, Berkeley

Harris B (1965b) Urban Development Models: New Tools for Planning. Journal of the American Institute of Planners 31

Harris B (1967) The limits of science and humanism in planning, Journal of American Institute of Planners 33

Harris B et al (1977) Urban Planning in Theory and Practice, Environment and Planning A, vol 9, 1977 and vol 10, 1978

Harsanyi JC (1978) Rule Utilitarianism and Decision Theory. In: Gottinger H, Leinfellner W (ed) Decision Theory and Social Ethics: Issues in Social Choice, Reidel, Dordrecht

Harvey D (1989). The condition of Postmodernity: An Enquiry into the Origin of Cultural Change. Oxford, Blackwell

Haveman RH (1970) Public Expenditures and Policy Analysis: An Overview. In: Haveman RH, Margolis J (ed) Public Expenditures and Policy Analysis, Markham Rand McNally, Chicago

Healey P, McDougall G, Thomas MJ (ed) (1982) Planning Theory: Prospects for the 1989s. Pergamon, Oxford

Healey P (1983) Local Plans in British Land-use Planning. Pergamon, Oxford

Healey P (1992) Planning Through Debate. The Communicative Turn in Planning Theory. Town Planning Review 63(2)

Healey P (1997) Collaborative Planning. Shaping Places in Fragmented Societies. London, Macmillan Press Ltd

Hill M (1973) Planning for Multiple Objectives: An Approach to the Evaluation of Transportation Plans, Regional Science Research Institute, University of Pennsylvania, Philadelphia

Hodgson GM (1988) Economics and Institutions: A Manifest for a Modern Institutional Economics. Polity Press, Oxford

Holland S (ed) (1978) Beyond Capitalist Planning. Basil Blackwell, Oxford

Hudson BM (1979) Comparison of Current Planning Theories: Counterparts and Contradictions. J APA 45(4)

Hudson B, Friedmann J (1973) Knowledge and Action: A Guide to Planning Theory. University of California, School of Architecture and Urban Planning, University of California, Los Angeles

Hutchinson TW (1964) Positive Economics and Policy Objectives. George Allen and Unwin, London

Innes JE (1995) Planning Theory's Emerging Paradigm: Communicative Action and the Interactive Practice. J Plan Educ Res 14(3):183–189

Isard W et al (1969) General Theory: Social, Political, Economic, and Regional, with Particular Reference to Decision-Making Analysis. MIT Press, Cambridge

Isard W (1960) Methods of Regional Analysis: An Introduction to Regional Science. MIT Press, New York

Johansen L (1977–1978) Lectures on Macroeconomic Planning. Vol. 1: A General Aspects. Vol. 2: Centralisation, Decentralisation, under Uncertainty Planning. North-Holland, Amsterdam

Juster FT, Land KC (ed) (1981) Social Accounting Systems. Essays on the State of the Art. Academic Press, New York

Kantorovich LV (1959) The Best Use of Economic Resources. Pergamon, London

Kaufmann A (1968) Le tecniche decisionali: introduzione alla praxeologia. Il Saggiatore, Milano

Khakee A (1998) Emerging Issues for Evaluation Theory. In: Lichfield N et al (eds) Evaluation in Planning: Facing the Challenge of Complexity. Kluwer Academic Press, Dordrecht

Khakee A (1998) The communicative turn in planning and evaluation. In: Lichfield N et al (eds) Evaluation in Planning: Facing the Challenge of Complexity. Kluwer Academic Press, Dordrecht

Kenney M (1995) Remember, Stonewall was a Riot: Understanding Gay and Lesbian Experience in the City. Plan Theory 13 (Summer 1995)

Kindler J, Kiss I (1984) Future Methodology Based on Post Assumption. In: Tomlinson R, Kiss I (eds) Rethinking the Process of Operational Research and Systems Analysis. Pergamon Press, Oxford

Koopmans TC (ed) (1951) Activity Analysis of Production and Allocation, Wiley, New York

Kotarbinski T (1965) Praxiology: An Introduction to Science of Efficient Action. Pergamon Press, Oxford

Kraushaar R, Gardels N (1982) Towards an Understanding of Crisis and Transition: Planning in an Era of Limits. In: Paris C (ed) Critical Readings in Planning Theory. Pergamon Press, Oxford

Kreukels AMJ (ed) (1982) The Planning Debate in the Netherlands. In: Planning and Development in the Netherlands XIV(1) Lakatos I, Musgrave A (ed) (1970) Criticism and Growth of Knowledge. Cambridge University Press, Cambridge

Kreukels AMJ (1983) Development in Strategic Planning: An Overview. Section for Urban and Regional Planning, Rijksuniversiteit Utrecht. Leontief W (1964) Modern Techniques for Economic Planning and Projections. In: Leontief W (ed) Essays in Economics, Vol 1, Theories and Theorizing. Blackwell, Oxford

Kuhn Th S (1962) The structure of scientific revolutions. University of Chicago Press, Chicago

Lakatos I, Musgrave A (eds) (1970) Criticism and Growth of Knowledge. Cambridge University Press, Cambridge

Leontief W (1966) Modern Techniques for Economic Planning and Projections. In: Leontief W (ed) Essays in Economics. Blackwell. Oxford 1:237–247

Leontief W (1974) Structure of the World Economy. Outline of a Simple Input-Output Formulation. Swed J Economics 76

Leontief W (1976) National Economic Planning; Methods and Problems. In: Leontief W (eds) The Economic System in a Age of Discontinuity. New York University Press, New York

Leontief W (1977) The Future of the World Economy. United Nations, New York

Lewis CI (1946) An Analysis of Knowledge and Valuation. Open Cour, La Salle

Lichfield N et al (1975) Evaluation in the Planning Process. Pergamon, Oxford

Lichfield D, Lichfield N (1992) The integration of environmental assessment and development planning. In: Project Appraisal, Sept. 1992, pp 175–185

Lichfield N (1996) Community Impact Evaluation. University College of London Press, London

Lichfield N et al (1998) Evaluation in Planning: Facing the Challenge of Complexity. Kluwer Academic Press, Dordrecht

Lichfield N (1998) Trends in Planning Evaluation: A British Perspective. In: Lichfield N et al (eds) Evaluation in Planning: Facing the Challenge of Complexity. Kluwer Academic Press, Dordrecht

Lichfield D (1998) Integrated planning and environmental impact assessment. In: Lichfield N et al (eds) Evaluation in Planning: Facing the Challenge of Complexity. Kluwer Academic Press, Dordrecht

Los M (1981 [1971]) Some reflexions on epistemology, design and planning theory. In: Dear M., Scott AJ (eds), Urbanization and Urban Planning Capitalist Society. Methuen, London-New York

Mandelbaum SJ (1979) A Complete General Theory of Planning is Impossible. Policy Sci 11(1):59–71

Mandelbaum SJ (1985) Historians and planners: the construction of pasts and futures. J APA 51:185–188

Mandelbaum SJ (1990) Reading Plans. J Am Plan Assoc 56:350–356

Mandelbaum SJ (1992) Telling Stories. J Plan Educ Res 10(3):209–214

Mandelbaum SJ (1993) Reading Old Plans. J Policy Hist 5(1):189–198

Mazza L (1995) Technical Knowledge, Practical Reason and the Planner Responsibility. Town Plan Rev 66:389–409

McKean RN (1958) Efficiency in Government Through Systems Analysis. Wiley, New York

McKean RN (1968) Public Spending. McGraw-Hill, New York

McLoughlin JB (1969) Urban and Regional Planning, A System Approach. Pergamon Press, Oxford

Mitchell WC (1935) The Social Sciences and National Planning. In: Science LXXXI, p 2090

Morris C (1956) Varieties of Human Value. University of Chicago Press, Chicago

Mueller DC (1989) Public Choice II (A Revised Edition). CUP, Cambridge

Myrdal G (1953) The Political Element in the Development of Economic Theory. Routledge & Paul, London

Myrdal G (1958) Value in Social Theory: a Selection of Essays on Methodology. Edited by Paul Streeten, Harper, New York 1958

Myrdal G (1960) Beyond the Welfare State: Economic Planning and its International Implications. Yale University Press, New Haven

Myrdal G (1969) Objectivity in Social Research. Pantheon Books, New York

Myrdal G (1972) How Scientific are the Social Sciences? Cahiers de l'ISEA, Serie H.S. 14

Myrdal G (1973) Against the Stream: Critical Essays on Economics. London, MacMillan.

National Resources Committee (1935) Regional Factors in National Planning and Development. National Resources Committee, Washington, DC

Nijkamp P, Voogd H (1985) An Informal Introduction to Multicriteria Evaluation. In: Fandel G, Spronk J (eds) Multiple Criteria Decision Methods and Application. Springer, Berlin Heidelberg New York

Nijkamp P et al (1990) Multiple Criteria Evaluation: Issues and Perspectives. In: Shefer D, Voogd H (eds) Evaluation Methods for Urban and Regional Planning, Pion, London

Nordhaus WD, Tobin J (1973) Is Growth Obsolete? In: Moss M (ed) The Measurement of Economic and Social Performance. Columbia University Press, New York

Novick D (ed) (1965) Program Budgeting: Program Analysis and the Federal Budget. Harvard University Press, Cambridge, MA

Oecd (1972) Educational Research and Innovation, Inter- Interdisciplinarity: Problems of Teaching and Research in University. OECD, Paris

Oecd (1973) List of Social Concerns Common to Most OECD Countries. OECD, Paris

Oecd (1976) Measuring Social Well-Being: A Progress Report on the Development of Social Indicators. OECD, Paris

Oecd (1982) The OECD List of Social Indicators. OECD, Paris

Olson M (1973) Evaluating Performance in the Public Sector. In: Moss M (ed) The Measurement of Economic and Social Performance. Columbia University Press, New York

Ozbekhan H (1969) Toward a General Theory of Planning. In: OECD, Perspectives of Planning. OECD, Paris

Papandreou AG, Zohar U (1971) Programme-Project Formulation, Evaluation and Selection in the Context of a National Plan. Econ Plan 11:1–2

Paris C (ed) (1982) Critical Readings in Planning Theory. Pergamon, Oxford

Parsons T (1937) The Social System. Glencoe, III: The Free Press

Parsons T, Shils EA (1951) Toward a General Theory of Action. Harvard University Press, Cambridge

Parsons T (ed) (1961) Theories of Society. The Free Press of Glencoe, III, Glencoe

Parsons T (1968) Systems Analysis: Social Systems. International Encyclopaedia of the Social Sciences, 15

Pettman BO (1977) Socio-Economic Systems. In: Pettman BO (ed) Social Economics: Concepts and Perspectives. MCB Book, Hull

Poxon J (1998) Exploring the hearth of the matter: the role of development plans in planning systems. (Paper presented to the XII AESOP Congress, July 1998, Aveiro, Portugal)

Rabinovitz F (1967) Politics, Personality and Planning. Public Administration Review 27

Rabinovitz F (1969) City Planning and Politics. Atherton Press, New York

Rittel HWJ, Webber MM (1973) Dilemmas in a General Theory of Planning. Policy Sci 4:155-169

Robbins L (1935) An Essay on the Nature and Significance of Economic Science. Macmillan, London

Salet WGM (1980) Planning Theory: The Quest for Identity. Working Paper n. 49. Utrecht, Instituut voor Planologie, Rijksuniversiteit Ultrecht

Scheele Rein (1982) Trias Planologica (working paper n 1 Utrecht, Instituut voor planologie, Rijksuniversiteit, pp 1-12

Schultze CL (1968) The Politics and Economics of Public Spending. Brookings Institution, Washington, DC

Schultze CL et al (1970) Setting National Priorities. The 1971 Budget. Brookings Institution, Washington, DC

Seebass G, Toumela A (ed) (1985) Social Action. Reidel, Dordrecht

Seers D (1972) The Prevalence of Pseudo-Planning. In: Faber M, Seers D (eds) The Crisis in Planning. Chatto & Windus, London

Sen AK (1970) Collective Choice and Social Welfare. Holden Day & Oliver, San Francisco

Sen AK (1982) Choice, Welfare and Measurement. Blackwell, Oxford

Sen AK (1986) Foundations of Social Choice Theory: An Epilogue. In: Elster J, Hylland A (eds) Foundations of Social Choice Theory. CUP, Cambridge

Seni DA (1996a) Planning as Sociotechnology. In: Kuklinski A (ed) Production of knowledge and the dignity of science. Rewasz Euroreg, Warsaw, pp 131-146

Seni DA (1996b) Planning Theory or the Theory of Plans? In: Kuklinski A (ed) Production of knowledge and the dignity of science production of knowledge and the dignity of science. Rewasz, Euroreg, Warsaw, pp 147-159

Simmie J (1989) A Preliminary Sketch of a Non-introverted Planning Theory. Plan Theory Newsl, n 2

Simon HA (1947) Administrative Behaviour. MacMillan, London

Simon HA (1957) Models of Man. Social and Rational. Wiley, New York

Simon HA (1969) The Sciences of the Artificial. MIT Press, Cambridge

Sinden JA, Worrell AC (1979) Unpriced Values: Decisions without Market Prices. Wiley, New York

Stone R et al (1959) Social Accounting and Economic Models. Bowes and Bowes, London

Stone R (1967) The Use of Social Accounting Matrices in Building Planning Models (mimeo). University of Cambridge, Cambridge

Taylor N (1984) A Critique of Materialist Critiques of Procedural Planning Theory, (with a comment by Scott AJ). Environ Plan B 11:103-126

Taylor N (1998) Urban Planning Theory since 1945. Sage, San Francisco

Terleckyi NE (1981) A Social Framework for Resources Accounting. In: Juster FT, Land KC (eds) Social Accounting Systems. Essays on the State of the Art. Academic Press, New York

Thomas H, Healey P (1991) Dilemmas of Planning Practice. Aldershot, Hants, Avebury

Thompson WR (1972) The National System of Cities as an Object of Public Policy. Urban Studies 9(1)

Thorgmorton JA (1993) Planning as a Rhetorical Activity. Am Plan Assoc J

Thorgmorton JA (1996) Planning as Paersuasive Storytelling. The University of Chicago Press, Chicago

Tinbergen J (1952) On the Theory of Economic Policy. North-Holland, Amsterdam

Tinbergen J (1956) Economic Policy; Principles and Design. North-Holland, Amsterdam

Tinbergen J (1964) Central Planning. Yale Univ. Press, New Haven

Tinbergen J (1966) Development Planning. McGraw Hill, New York

Tinbergen J (1968) Wanted; A World Development Plan. In: International Organization, XXII

Tinbergen J (1971a) Comment faut-il étudier l'avenir?, (roneo) 1971

Tinbergen J (1971b) Two Approaches to the Future: Planning vs. Forecasting. (roneo), 1971

Tomlinson R (1984) Rethinking the Process of Systems Analysis and Operational Research: From Practice to Precept and Back Again. In: Tomlinson R, Kiss I (ed) Rethinking the Process of Operational Research and Systems Analysis. Pergamon Press, Oxford, pp 205–223

Tomlinson R, Kiss I (ed) (1984) Rethinking the Process of Operational Research and Systems Analysis. Pergamon Press, Oxford

United Nations, ECOSOC (1970) Resolution 1491 (XLVIII), Politique et planification sociale dans le développement national, 26 Mai 1970

United Nations, Economic Commission for Europe (1975) Use of Systems of Models in Planning. Papers to the Seminar on the 'Use of Models in Planning', Moscow 2–11 December 1974, United Nations, New York

United Nations, General Assembly (1970) Resolution 2681 (XXV): Conception unifiée de la planification économique et sociale dans le développement national (11 December 1970)

United Nations, Statistical Office (1975) Towards a System of Social and Demographic Statistic, Report by R. Stone. United Nations, New York

UNRISD (1975) Report on a Unified Approach to Development Analysis and Planning (5-12-1974) (24th Session of the UN Commission for Social Development, 6–24 January 1975)

UNRISD (1980) The Quest for a Unified Approach to Development, with an Assessment by Marshall Wolfe. Geneva, Switzerland

US Congress, Joint Economic Committee (1969) The Analysis and Evaluation of Public Expenditures: the PPB system. US GPO, Washington, DC

US Advisory Committee on National Growth Policy Processes (1977) Forging America's Future: Strategies for National Growth and Development. Government Printing Office, Washington, DC

Verma N (1996) Pragmatic Rationality and Planning Theory. J Plan Educ Res 16:(5–14)

Vettoretto L (1996) Planning Theory and Fragmented Society, Explorations into Melvin Webber's Civic Liberalism. In: Planning Theory 17:113–141

Voogd H (1983) Multicriteria Evaluation for Urban and Regional Planning. Pion Limited, London

Voogd H (1998) The communicative ideology and ex ante planning evaluation. In: Lichfield N et al (eds) Evaluation in Planning: Facing the Challenge of Complexity. Kluwer Academic Press, Dordrecht

Waterston A (1965) Development Planning, Lesson of Experience. John Hopkins Press, Baltimore

Webber MM (ed) (1964) Explorations into Urban Structure. University of Pennsylvania Press, Philadelphia

Webber MM (1978) A Difference Paradigm for Planning. In: Burchell RW, Sternlieb G (ed) Planning Theory in the 1980's. A Search for Future Directions. Rutgers University, New Jersey

Wheaton WC (1974) A Comparative Static Analysis of Urban Spatial Structure. J Econ Theory (9):223–237

Wildavsky A (1973) If Planning is Everything, Maybe It's Nothing. Policy Sci 4:127–153

Wilson AG (1968) Models in Urban Planning a Synoptic Review of Recent Literature. Urban Studies: 249–276

Wilson AG (1974) Urban and Regional Models in Geography and Planning. Wiley, London

Wilson T (1964) Planning and Growth. London, Macmillan & Co. Ltd

Woods C (1995) The Blues Epistemology and Regional Planning History. The Case of the Lower Mississippi Delta Development Commission. Plan Theory (13)

Yeechong W (1984) Ideology, Tradition and Social Development: A Study in Critical & Hermeneutical Theories of Planning. UBC Planning papers. School of Community and Regional Planning, Vancouver, July

Authors Index

A

Ackoff, R.L. 32n
Adorno, T.H. 8n
Albrecht, L. 18n, 100n, 101n, 102n
Alexander, E.R. Vn, VIn, VII, *10–14*, 26, 58n, 71n, 84n, 100n, 102n
Allmendinger, Ph. 3, 100n
Archibugi, F. 3n, 9n, 17n, 20n, 33n, 34, 38, 42, 50n, 51, 51n, 52n, 59n, 62n, 66n, 67n, 74, 75n, 76n, 77n, 81n, 89n, 95n, 96n
Aristotle 4n
Arrow, K.J. 33n, 60n

B

Baier, K. 86n,
Banfield, E.C. 4, 7, 10, 10n, 11
Barbanente, A. 89n
Batty, M. 89n
Baumeister, R. 23n, 25n
Baumol, W. 32n
Beauregard, R.A. 19n
Bellman, R.E. 32n
Benli, Ö.M. 23n
Benveniste, G. 10n
Berkman, H.G. 20
Borri, D. 89
Breheny, M. 89n
Bryson, J. Vn, VIn
Buchanan, J.M. 33n
Burchell, R.W. 1n

C

Campbell, S. 1n

Catanese, J.A. 62n
Chadwick, G. 2n, 62n, 88n, 89n
Chapin, F.S. 18
Checkland, P.B. 56n, 57n
Churchmann, C.W. 32n, 56n
Commons, J.R. 8n
Comte, A. 8n, 31
Condorcet, Marquis de 8n, 22
Considerant, V. 31n
Cooke, P. VIII, 62n

D

Dantzig, G.B. 32n
Darin-Drabkin, H. 20
Delors, J. 52n
De Luca, G. Vn, VIn
Denayer, W. 100n, 101n
Dennis, N. 10n
Dewey, J. 8n, 59n
Dorfman, R. 32n
Doxiades, K.A. 18
Drewnowski, J. 49
Dror, Y. 10n, 33n
Durkheim, E. 8n
Dyckman, J. 11, 20, 64n

E

Etzioni, A. 10n

F

Faludi, A. VIII, *2–6*, 10n, 17, 17n, 20, 23, 26, 38n, 55n, 60n, 62, 62n, 97, 97n, *90–100*
Farago, L. 2n, 23n, 102n, 104n

Analytical Index

Printed in November 2007